London Relocation Guide: Insider Tips for a Smooth Move

Kieren .W Simmons

All rights reserved. Copyright © 2023 Kieren .W Simmons

Funny helpful tips:

Consistency is key in any fitness regimen; it's the daily dedication that leads to long-term results and transformations.

Your essence is a blend of experiences; cherish each one, knowing they mold your character.

*London Relocation Guide: Insider Tips for a Smooth Move :
The Essential Handbook for an Effortless London Relocation:
Expert Advice and Secrets for a Seamless Move*

Life advices:

Prioritize mental exercises; activities like puzzles and reading enhance cognitive function and memory.

Practice mutual encouragement; uplift each other in all endeavors.

Introduction

This book offers a personal and insightful perspective on the expatriate experience, particularly for those relocating to the United Kingdom. The memoirs, along with practical survival tips, provide a comprehensive guide for individuals and families making the transition to life in the UK.

The journey begins with "Moving In," recounting the author's own experience of becoming a Londoner. This section delves into the emotional and logistical aspects of moving to a new country, capturing the challenges and joys of adapting to a foreign land.

Language is a fundamental aspect of integration, and "Languages" provides valuable insights into mastering the English language, often dubbed the language of Shakespeare. The author shares advice on language acquisition and highlights the importance of effective communication in daily life.

For those considering higher education in the UK, "University" offers a glimpse into the educational opportunities available. It discusses the pursuit of academic dreams and offers practical information about studying in British universities.

"Job Hunting" provides a candid look at the struggles and successes of seeking employment as an expatriate. It offers guidance on overcoming challenges and navigating the job market, ensuring that readers are well-prepared for their own job-hunting endeavors.

"Housing" explores the concept of home and its significance in the expatriate experience. From finding suitable accommodation to creating a sense of belonging, this section offers advice on settling into a new place.

"Life" delves into the essence of being a Londoner, offering readers a glimpse into the unique lifestyle, culture, and experiences that come with residing in the UK's vibrant capital. It paints a vivid picture of life in London.

"Addresses" is a practical section, providing information on essential addresses and resources that expatriates may need during their stay. It offers valuable insights into navigating daily life in the UK.

Brexit, a significant event in recent history, is addressed in the section "Brexit." The author discusses the UK's decision to leave the European Union and the potential implications for expatriates, providing a comprehensive overview of this complex issue.

Finally, "Moving Back" delves into the idea of returning to one's roots after the expatriate journey. It offers reflections on the author's own experience of going back and provides essential information for those considering a similar move.

This book combines personal stories with practical advice, making it an invaluable resource for individuals and families planning to move to the UK. It offers a holistic view of the expatriate experience, from the emotional challenges of relocation to the practicalities of daily life, ensuring that readers are well-prepared for their own adventures in the United Kingdom.

Contents

1. Moving In 1
   How we became the Londoners 2
   What you need to know 10
2. Languages 14
   Mastering the language of Shakespeare.......................15
   What you need to know 27
   The IELTS exam 29
3. University 34
   Following the dream...35
   What you need to know 43
4. Job Hunting...47
   Struggles can be overcome 48
   What you need to know 57
5. Housing 62
   Home is where the heart is...63
   What you need to know 71
6. Life 75
   What it means to be Londoners...76
   What you need to know 83
   Addresses...87
7. Brexit 93
   They voted out..94
   What you need to know 97
8. Moving Back 98
   Going back to our roots...99
   What you need to know 104
Every adventure has an end, or has it? 105

1. Moving In

How we became the Londoners

Until we actually moved, the whole thing felt surreal.

"Do you both speak English?" Quentin's grandmother would ask, each time we visited.

"Yes, we do," he'd answer.

I didn't have Quentin's confidence in the language, however I was slowly getting there – but more on that in the next chapter. We had done all the paperwork, ordered a Visa credit card and booked our one-way train tickets and first month of Airbnb. If you're not familiar with the concept of Airbnb, it's a way for people to rent out a room they're not using to people visiting the area. Our prospective room was located around Barkingside tube station, on the Central Line.

Our families and friends may have found it hard to believe, but we were ready. We had decided beforehand that we'd stay in London for three months as a test. If neither of us found a job, we'd come back after the test.

But we weren't going to fail, were we?

On our mums' advice, we had gone on a farewell tour. Not everyone understood why we were doing this. To some, we were foolish to even think that we would make it. Our dream wasn't enough. I could detect a hint of jealousy lurking in the dark. Fortunately, most people were supportive of our project, even if they wouldn't have wanted to do it themselves. The idea seemed scary to them. And we could understand that, since we were feeling the same way!

On the eve of our departure, we proposed a toast to the adventure ahead of us. We didn't know how long we would stay in the UK, nor when we'd see our loved ones again. We weren't going to the other side of the world: it is a mere 356km between London and our

Belgian hometown. However, Eurostar – the only train provider connecting Brussels to London – was a tad expensive for our small budget.

On a cold morning in February 2015, we hugged our mums one last time before entering the Eurostar check-in area at Brussels Midi train station. My cheeks were red from holding my tears back – I'm naturally emotional. From now on, it was only going to be the two of us and our suitcases full of clothes, hopes and dreams.

Brussels to London takes only two hours by train, so we arrived at St-Pancras International far too fast for my taste. But I was still excited at embarking on our project. We had talked about what we would do once in London: visiting all the parks and tourist attractions, and discovering all the different cuisines – other than French and Italian, which are pretty common in Belgium. However, as I set foot on the platform at St-Pancras, I felt overwhelmed by our main task: becoming Londoners. I had been to London before, for shopping and language courses – which I had always done on my own, not always willingly. The city wasn't so scary when you were a tourist, because you were only there for a couple of days. But we weren't tourists any more.

It was one of those sunny days in London, surprisingly. We had heard so many things about London before moving, and people think it rains all the time. I can assure you it doesn't rain as much as in Belgium. Every time I had my mum on the phone, it was raining on her end while it was a bright, sunny day on mine.

I protected my eyes with one hand, looking up at the buildings. We were in a megalopolis now, nothing comparable with the Belgian countryside, where houses aren't even as tall as five or six metres. But I wouldn't be able to enjoy the sun for a while: we had to go underground and take the tube.

Barkingside is in East London, in "zone four". The capital is spread out in different zones for the purpose of the transport systems: the further you are from the centre, the higher the zone number – and the higher the tube fares. Quentin and I were going to be living in the fourth zone (out of nine), at least for a month.

As we walked out of Barkingside tube station, I shook my head, surprised we had arrived at the rendezvous point so quickly... and worried that there was nobody to greet us! We were a long way out of Central London, literally in the middle of nowhere. I have to admit that I was a little scared – if I hadn't already been. What if nobody was coming? What if we'd made it all the way for nothing? But then a tall middle-aged man wearing a red jumper arrived at the station. He was all relaxed smiles.

"Hope you had a safe journey. My name is Adrian, welcome to London."

Oh gosh! All I could do was smile and nod. I was still terrified to speak to a British person. I thought that as soon as he heard my accent, he would make fun of me – it was all in my head, of course.

Adrian took our luggage to his car, Quentin and I followed him and found a second surprise. Britons, unlike continental Europeans, drive on the left side of the road. When I tried to sit in the driver's seat, he laughed. My hands became wet and I blushed. It seemed so unnatural to me, still is to this day. I went to the rear, leaving the front seat to Quentin. I kept looking through the window all the way to Adrian's, scared we would collide with another car. And, as a driver myself, my feet kept moving on their own, on a non-existent pedal as if I could somehow slow the car down.

Our Airbnb turned out to be a white detached house in a residential area in Ilford. We were shown into a little ground-floor room, with a mini-fridge, a bed and a wardrobe. It was located at the front of the house, so we had a view of the street and the trees. Our host said we could use the kitchen, the living room and the downstairs bathroom. We were already starting to feel at home.

Adrian had prepared a welcome dinner on the first night. I don't remember every detail, but it was very typical of the British cuisine. We discovered that he was a lawyer living alone with his teenage daughter.

"I love having people around," he explained. "It's mind-opening to listen to their stories and get to know their cultures."

Quentin and I grinned: this was just the beginning of our own adventure.

We started to apply for jobs right away and, believe it or not, he was offered one after sending out just one or two CVs. And nailing the job interviews, of course. Because Quentin was a front-end developer, I felt like he had just been able to click his fingers and be handed any job in the world. We celebrated his success at a nearby Italian restaurant, decorated with Robert De Niro's pictures. At that point it all seemed so easy for him while I was still struggling with my own unemployment and insecurities.

One day, I heard of an event organised by a career coach at an All Bar One in Central London, so I went. The theme was *How To Create A Kick-Ass CV*, which I was sure was my weakness.

"British CVs are different from French ones. For instance, there's no photo of yourself on it. That is because companies try to avoid discrimination based on someone's look," he said.

I kept nodding and taking notes.

At the end of the session, the coach explained he would be organising more. I gave him my contact details, like the other attendees. Well, let me give you this advice: it's not always a good thing to give your contact details to a career coach. I had barely left the session when he texted me the price of his private one-on-one. When I made it clear I wasn't interested – it was a tad expensive – he made me feel guilty.

"You'll never find a job in the UK without me," he said.

What a wonderful career coach!

And because I love proving people wrong, I was actually invited to my first interview a couple of days later: a media company in Southwark. I had a lot more interviews, but that first one was the toughest. I had prepared for it, so I was able to recite some answers I had learned by heart. In retrospect, it was the best and the worst thing I had ever experienced. The worst because I couldn't understand the interviewers very well, I had to ask them to repeat things... a lot! The best because I was coming from a job in which I wasn't valued. And here I was, being considered for a proper role within a prestigious company.

I got a rejection, of course, but just getting the interview meant a lot.

As Quentin prepared himself for his new job, I wanted to do something useful with my time, like volunteering. I didn't want to stay home doing nothing but blaming myself for not landing a job. But to volunteer – and to work at all in the UK – I needed a National Insurance Number, or NIN for short. I prepared one or two sentences that I could read out loud in the hope that the person on the other end would understand me. Then I called the Job Centre – where you could get this famous number – to set up a meeting.

I ended up at Whitechapel's Job Centre. You know, Whitechapel, where Jack the Ripper used to do his killing... No big deal.

Usually, you go to the nearest Job Centre. But as I had called to get a meeting, they assigned me to Whitechapel, even though it wasn't in the same area as Ilford at all. Or was it because they were the only one who dealt with National Insurance Numbers? I honestly don't remember.

Anyhow, the area felt a bit unreal. The tube station was a labyrinth of tunnels and stairs. When I dragged myself out of it, the journey did not end there. The route to the Job Centre was tedious but fortunately I had a brilliant phone app called Citymapper. If you don't have it already, I recommend it. It saved me so many times: I never got lost in London after I had downloaded it.

I arrived at the Job Centre and waited for my turn. A small middle-aged blonde lady called the next person. But I couldn't tell if she was genuinely calling me or someone else. The pronunciation was so wrong: "Vivaldi?" she asked.

"It's more Van de Velde, but yes, that's me."

"Doesn't matter," she barked.

Needless to say that the meeting started pretty badly. She kept asking me why I wanted a National Insurance Number and I kept answering that it was for volunteering, in a continuous loop. I thought she was never going to accept my application but, in the end, I received it by post after a couple of days.

After a month in London, we asked Adrian if we could extend our stay. We had gotten along well and it would have been easier for us to stay where we were instead of moving house.

"I'm truly sorry, guys, but I can't let you stay," Adrian replied.

He was planning on redoing the downstairs bathroom – the one we were using – and the heavy work was planned for right after our departure date. We were disappointed, of course, but we understood.

We quickly found another Airbnb in Leytonstone, still on the Central Line, in "zone three". After packing our things and saying goodbye to Adrian, we knocked on the door of what we thought would be another family.

But it wasn't...

An estate agent – apparently Russian – greeted us. Our room was located on the first floor of a dirty house, and it wasn't ready at all. There was a mattress on the floor, and absolutely nothing else. Where had the feeling of being home gone?

The rest of the house matched up. The kitchen was a mess of filthy utensils and saucepans. We wouldn't be able to cook anything unless we washed them twice beforehand (at least)! We would be sharing the house with two or three other couples, and I couldn't help but cry in despair. The situation was catastrophic in my eyes: we had already paid for a month, I had no job, no friends and no family. The feeling of being somewhere you just shouldn't be was so overwhelming.

Quentin started his new job in a medical tech-company, leaving me alone with my thoughts, my uncertainties and job applications. His job was in Central London, near Farringdon. However, it meant we would soon be able to rent our own place – the light at the end of the tunnel.

After a week, the Russian moved us to another, cleaner house near Leytonstone. It was in a residential area, not far from the previous place. We shared it with a Greek couple, who were lovely people. Our bedroom was even smaller than the previous one: it could barely fit a bed – but at least there was a bed this time! The house felt warmer and more homely.

I didn't realise it yet, but at this stage, we had made it. It was April 2015, two months into our three-month test period. One of us had got a job in the UK. We had officially become "the Londoners".

What I would do in the next months was still unknown, but my next task would be to find us a place to live.

Spoiler alert: it's also an adventure on its own!

What you need to know

Moving to another country can be daunting from an emotional point of view. But how about from an administrative point of view?

When we talk about expatriation or emigration, we often think of the paperwork that needs to be completed to move countries. I am going to explain what we had to do, but keep in mind we moved from Belgium to the United Kingdom, which were both part of the European Union at the time – the UK has officially left the EU as of January 2020. The B-word sucks...

Before moving

• Make sure **your IDs are in order**. Quentin and I just needed an ID card, but you might need a passport and/or a visa. Those things take a long time to arrange, so be aware of the time you need to have those essential papers in order.

• If you're unemployed, you might be able to **keep your country's benefits** for a couple of months. I was unemployed at the time, and I was getting benefits from Belgium. To keep my rights in the UK, I had to meet my Belgian counsellor in my home city (before we moved, of course) and fill in an administrative paper, called a **B2 form**. It enabled me to continue receiving benefits from Belgium for three months after I arrived in the UK. However, after those three months, I knew I would be on my own. You might have to do the same in your country, so do your research carefully.

• Financially, Quentin and I had made sure that we were able to **support ourselves for at least three to four**

months without a job, by saving money before we left. It helped us a great deal when looking for our first flat. I recommend that you do this too.

• In Belgium, we pay by card with Maestro cards, which don't work internationally. So we **ordered a Visa card** from our bank (this can also take time to arrive).

• Get your **international health insurance** in order. The UK has a great National Health Service (NHS) that is free for everyone. But getting doctor's appointments can be a long wait, unless you're going to the hospital accident and emergency wards. Just in case you'd need something urgent, it's always good to have your insurance in good shape.

• You can either **book a hotel room or an Airbnb**, whichever you prefer. We went with Airbnb because it was cheaper than the hotel. Our criteria: price, location, pictures and reviews.

On the spot

You arrived in the country, congratulations! Maybe take a day or two to adjust to your new situation, you deserve it. There are a couple of things you need to do to settle in:

• First, you need a **mobile phone number** from the country. Quentin and I went with Giffgaff. It was the easiest solution: you could order it online without needing to prove your address or anything. The SIM card arrived at our Airbnb, and it was prepaid. There are, of course, a lot of other mobile phone providers (EE, O2, etc.) and you can choose the one you think fits best. You are also free to go to a shop if you would rather talk to a human being rather than ordering it online, it is totally up to you.

• A **local bank account** might be the second step. If you already have a job in your new country, it would be better if they could pay you for your hard work, wouldn't it? In the UK, you can't open a bank account if you don't have proof of address. We bypassed that with our... SIM card, yes that's right. As Giffgaff had sent us our SIM card by post, we had an "official" letter stating our address in the country. With that in hand, we went to Lloyds Bank and opened an expat bank account. You may want to get more information about the different banks though. Every one of them has their particular pros and cons and one may be better for your own needs than another.

• If you'd like to **transfer money** to or from your brand new bank account, you may use Transferwise (now called Wise). It reduces the exchange costs and works faster than any bank. I used it to transfer euros into pounds, and vice versa.

• What about your **unemployment benefits**? In the UK, you'll have to register with the nearest Job Centre with that paper you obtained from your country's administration. Once you register with them, they'll contact your home country's administration. You might then be able to continue claiming your country's benefits for a limited amount of time – it worked for me because I'm an EU citizen, but after Brexit I don't know if the agreement still holds. However, once it's finished, you might not be able to claim your new country's benefits. Once again: make sure you do your research (Brexit might affect the paperwork for that one too).

• When you're ready to work, you will also need a **National Insurance Number** (NIN). It is simply a number that is allocated to you for tax and other purposes. Where do you get it in the UK? From that very same Job Centre.

2. Languages

Mastering the language of Shakespeare

In 1999 in my tiny part of the world, students starting high school had three language options: English, Dutch or German. I was eleven, so I didn't think about it too hard. I chose the (arguably) most international one.

The first year was a blast. My teacher, a silver-haired woman with a kind smile, made us perform little plays in class and my grades were excellent. I learned that "Brian is in the kitchen" and "he's in love with Sue". But in the second year, it became more complicated to get good grades. We were having to get to know the past tense and the irregular verbs list.

That list and I aren't good friends.

English wasn't fun anymore. The silver-haired teacher had been replaced by a younger, inflexible, short-haired woman. Unfortunately for me, the new vocabulary and irregular verbs list just wouldn't stick in my head: they went in one ear and out the other.

My mum tried to help me, every night for half an hour with *What You Must Know*, a French-English book for students... which meant even more lists of words to master.

"How do you say *bonjour* in English?"

"*Hello.*"

"What's the irregular of *to bring*?"

" ... "

"And what does it mean?"

"*Apporter!*"

The teacher tested us almost every day on the verbs we were supposed to have learned the day before. I always started the lesson with a stone in my chest because I knew, deep down, I wasn't going to make it. My grades were average, just enough so I'd pass. But what a change compared to the first year!

One day in class, things took a more dramatic turn. My parents were on holiday in Mexico for two weeks, so my sisters and I were being looked after by my maternal grandparents. I had received a couple of English tests I needed my mum to sign – the grades weren't pretty – and I asked my grandpa to sign them for her. They had the same name, and I thought the teacher wouldn't see the difference.

She called me out after class, brandishing the tests:

"Did you sign them?" she said.

"No, I didn't. My grandpa did, my mum's in Mexico."

"Liar! I'm calling your parents."

The word was out: I was a liar. I was twelve years old, and an authority figure had spat it right in my face.

"Your daughter is hopeless and arrogant!" the teacher told my mum at the next parents' meeting.

I wasn't there, which I would always be grateful for. But my mum repeated those words to me: she couldn't believe what she had just heard. She had blocked out the word "arrogant", and didn't listen to the "hopeless" part, but it still hurt. I'm older now, and I can't believe how heartless that particular teacher was. I don't know if teachers and professors always realise how heavy and important their words are. They can push a child up to the top or down to hell in seconds.

What was the point in making an effort to learn English if I was "hopeless"?

I lost all interest. I had that English teacher for only a year, but I spent the rest of high school seeing languages as a way to torture me.

I was thirteen or fourteen when my parents forced me to go to an English summer camp in the UK with Education First (EF). It was somewhere near Warwick or Luton. I only had three friends at school – I wasn't highly sociable – and now I was being pushed to spend two weeks with a group of teens I didn't know.

The integration didn't go very well. We had class in the morning and activities in the afternoon. Not a single word – from any language – was coming out of my mouth. I was so stubborn. We would each come back to our host family in the evening. I lived with a sweet old couple who, I am sure, tried to make my stay as comfortable and easy as possible. But I had made it clear that I didn't want to learn or improve.

It wasn't quite as awful as I am depicting it though. I remember going to a flea market with my hostess, meeting a couple of friends of theirs and having a good time. I tried to teach them a song by the French group *Kyo* and we watched the movie *Jaws* together.

After the stay, my parents decided to hire a private teacher. In fact they hired two – not at the same time, of course. But it was useless because I was doing it unwillingly. By the time I turned eighteen, I had successfully avoided all the third and fourth languages I could have gotten into. It was hopeless, remember?

I had set my heart on a scientific career and started medical studies at university, with no English on the programme – which was silly, considering English is the language of science.

I didn't have particular issues with language courses at university, even after I got into journalism, or when I had to master English AND Dutch to pass on to the next year. I could barely have a small conversation when I graduated. My parents gave up at some point and stopped bothering me more than necessary. I didn't have fantastic grades in English, but I wasn't failing either. So it worked out just about well enough for them.

At this stage, you may be wondering: how did I become fluent in English, if it was so difficult?

Quentin happened.

When he asked me to move to London, he gave me a choice. He was going to London, with or without me. The question was: would I follow him? I was completely in love with him – and the feeling was mutual! – and I couldn't bear the thought of ending the relationship for this reason. If I wasn't able to make the jump for him, then it couldn't be love, right?

"Do you speak English?"

When people asked us that very question, I used to cringe a lot. Because I didn't. Not to the standard I felt I needed to set myself anyway: I wasn't fluent, I spent too much time searching for words and I stammered as a result. I was being too hard on myself, but my uncertainties made it hard for anyone to believe I could do it.

As soon as it was clear we were moving to London, I started seriously learning the language. And when I say "seriously", I don't mean watching movies and TV shows with English subtitles on Netflix. I had resigned from my first job because I was feeling burned out, but I was still eager to take classes. It was July 2014, and I naturally turned to the Forem for support.

Just so you're not lost: Forem is an organisation which tries to help people to find a job. It's the equivalent to Pôle Emploi if you're French, or the Job Centre if you're British.

Before joining any English class, I had to pass a language test. One day, I pushed my way through the local Forem office's doors and waited in a tiny white-walled room before getting into the test zone. Sitting in front of an old-fashioned computer with an outdated version of Windows and an old screen – the kind of screen that would make a teenager recoil or mock – was the beginning of a harrowing experience.

The computer was shouting English questions at me, to which it supposed I knew the answers: grammar, spelling, listening test, you name it. The more I answered well, the more difficult the questions became. I didn't know a lot at that time. I was only armed with my 6+ years of English courses, two to three years of private teaching and one stay in the UK during summer. And after all that, Brian was still in his damn kitchen... So disappointing when you think of it.

Back in the white-walled room after the writing test, I waited my turn for the speaking part of the exam. A silver-haired woman called me in and we talked. As with any examination, my heart was racing. I was sure I had failed the writing part, so why bother?

A1: False beginner

I looked at the paper stating I would be in the beginner's class – all these years of struggle for that.

So I joined Véronique's class. She was a kind, silver-haired woman with a lot of energy and enthusiasm – it seems I may have a thing for silver-haired teachers. When you entered the room, you could feel that she had a deep love for the language of Shakespeare. And she was passing that on to her students. The class was made up of about ten people, all of us wanting more than our "lives as usual". We studied English together for two months (August and September 2014) and I am sure we made tremendous progress. But I wanted to study more. I didn't want to make "huge" progress: it needed to be "incredible". Not far from my place, a translator in his thirties had decided to organise roundtables for those who needed to practise their English. For over two months, I didn't miss any of these sessions.

I retook the test at the end of the course. It felt like I had improved, of course, but not to the point where I would be able to live and work in London.

A2: Advanced beginner

Could do better!

Things were going too slowly in Belgium. Quentin and I had planned to make the big move in February 2015, and I was a long way from reaching my goals. If I wanted to make significant improvements, I really needed to jump off the cliff – metaphorically speaking.

The Forem offered grants for immersion courses in London and Cambridge. This would cover my expenses, the price of the school I chose and the accommodation. I didn't think twice: I booked a train ticket to London.

However, I realised it was the first time Quentin and I would have been apart for more than a week. Watching the movie *Interstellar* the day before leaving didn't help. It's the story of a father who goes on a journey to space and returns to his daughter, who turned out to be on her deathbed while he hadn't aged at all. It's a beautiful movie. But I cried my eyes out thinking that a month apart would be terrible. Silly old me.

On an evening in November 2014, I dragged my suitcase from St Pancras to Southfields on the District Line. I met my new British family, who had been kind enough to offer to let me stay with them for a month while I went to The Burlington School of English, in an attempt to learn their language. The school was located on the District Line as well, at Parsons Green, which was three stops away.

I wasn't the only foreigner in the house: Bakhytzhan (alias Bakka), from Kazakhstan, had arrived a month or so before. I befriended him quickly: he showed me the area, and we visited quite a few places together. Among them, Richmond Park was my favourite.

Ah, Richmond Park... it's a vast park in South West London, in which you can rent a bike and see deer roaming around free. With my new friend, I cycled around the park for around an hour, maybe more. We took pictures with a stag that was chilling – at a safe distance, of course – and we went up the highest hill of the park to get a view over London. It was an amazing day, and I still have vivid memories of it. If you ever have the chance to visit London, I can't recommend you enough to go there, rent a bike and just cycle around the park.

At school, I also met Heesun, from South Korea, and Tomomi, from Japan – who ended up visiting me in Belgium in January 2015. All four of us got along well and discovered the city together. The Burlington School of English had a good programme, and I felt I was improving a lot. This was partly because I was always talking with my new friends and the family who I was staying with. The mum was a librarian so, obviously, we talked about books a lot.

This immersion course felt so different from the one I had done when I was fourteen. I could finally see the good in experiencing such a programme.

Was it worth it?

When I came back to Belgium, I took the infamous English test yet again.

B1: Intermediate level

I was so happy I had moved up a level. Quentin and I went to the restaurant that day, to celebrate around a pizza. At that very moment, I had good enough English to follow him wherever he wanted to go.

But did you think I'd stop my progress there?

One of the first times we went out of Adrian's place, we went to a McDonalds near Oxford Street.

"What can I get you?" the waitress said.

I was paralysed. I couldn't say a thing: my mouth had decided to stop functioning and my brain had gone blank. I couldn't believe it. I had been doing so well in the past couple of months, but now I wasn't even able to order a simple thing at McDonald's!

So I decided to go back to university. When I tell you that all you need to get the motivation is a goal, I am not kidding. We were in May 2015, and I wanted to enrol for September's academic year. What an adventure!

In the United Kingdom, you have to "apply" to universities to get in. One of the conditions for foreigners is to pass the IELTS test with a minimum level of a band 7. At that time, I was a 5.

If you don't know, IELTS stands for International English Language Testing System. It's an English test for someone for whom English isn't their first language – someone like me, maybe like you too.

I had four months to pass it with flying colours.

Following my usual habit, I bought a book. *Cambridge English's Complete IELTS: Bands 6.5-7.5* was supposed to help me pass the test. But I soon realised it wouldn't be enough. I don't know about you, but I find it challenging for me to study alone. Being motivated on your own all day... that's hard.

Early in June 2015, I enrolled for a five-week intensive English course at the Westminster Adult Education Service. I had registered online when looking for a way to prepare for the IELTS exam. The school was located around Piccadilly Circus and, with the help of the talented Jane, a tall short-haired teacher, I felt I was tipping the odds in my favour.

Now I wasn't studying alone: I was part of a group of eight people. Jane explained the different parts of IELTS (for more on this, see later in the chapter), and how to approach each of them. The exam had strict rules and timing so it was important for me to get this information and understand how it worked. We took fake tests each week for the reading, listening and writing parts, but not the speaking part, which terrified me. I didn't have great confidence in my speaking skills, even in French – my mother tongue!

At the Westminster Adult Education Service, I felt fully supported in every way. For instance, I was reading a book in English for one of my university applications, *Jonathan Strange & Mr Norrell* by Susanna Clarke. It's one big book of 1,000 pages: Jane looked impressed when I showed her.

"Reading literature will definitely help you get better with the language," she told me.

Just as I had combined the Forem's course with an English roundtable in Belgium, I decided I would consolidate my IELTS preparation course with an English meetup group, where I had the opportunity to practice speaking with people who were also struggling. I found one at Kentish Town Library.

And eventually the big day arrived...

I took the test on the 25th July 2015 at Regent's University, at the heart of Regent's Park. It was a peculiar experience, to say the least.

I had to go through a lot of identity checks before even sitting the test. One person took a photo of me, another took my fingerprints (yes!). I was then dispatched to an exam room where they rechecked my identity. It seemed a little overkill. As if someone could switch places with me within the exam room... I would have loved to be able to, though. I was so scared, my hands and feet were damp with sweat.

There was no break between the listening, reading and writing parts of the test. You needed to ask someone to come with you if you went to the bathroom. Yes, they were strict. There was no opportunity to chat with your neighbour either. And if that wasn't enough: they continued to check identities during the exam! I didn't move from my seat for two hours straight, but they seemed to be assuming I could have been replaced through some magic trick. Maybe I could have used teleportation powers, you never know.

After the first three parts, the examiners gave us the timetable for the speaking part. As my last name starts with a V, I had assumed that, as usual, I would end up in the last group. It was just the opposite: I was among the first ones called.

When I entered the room, I was alone with the examiner. I was stressed as hell. I don't like oral exams, I always think I am doing badly. I tried to talk as calmly as possible, without hesitation and with enthusiasm. However, I didn't think much of my performance.

After the test, I was hugely relieved. I had done it all, and I could finally rest a little.

Fast forward two weeks, when my results were available to be picked up. It felt like there was a rock in my stomach, and I could barely speak. Quentin's sister, Sophie, was staying with us for a week, visiting London. She was kind enough to come with me to discover my fate.

The moment I had dreaded for weeks had finally arrived. What if I had failed? I was already envisioning myself having to take the test a second time – I was that confident in my language skills. But Sophie took my hand, seeing I was stressing out a bit too much.

We arrived at the station and crossed a bridge. The building was coral-walled, but that's all I remember. I gave my ID card to the person in charge of delivering the results. Shaking, I took the envelope containing the results. I smiled at Sophie, to give me courage as I opened it.

My eyes went wide. With happiness.

C1: Advanced speaker

I couldn't believe my eyes. In less than a year, I had gone from false beginner to advanced speaker. The thought that this might be someone else's results immediately crossed my mind, but when I looked it was definitely my picture on the paper.

I had been judged fluent in English.

In English!

If only my high school teacher could see me now...

With a result of band 7.5, it was more than enough for me to attend university. All my efforts had finally paid off! I was so relieved, so happy. I couldn't help but smile, for real this time. I called Quentin and my mum right away to tell them the good news, and their joy matched mine.

I would love to go back in time and tell my younger self that she has no reason not to believe in herself. I would love to tell her that languages are an important part of her future, that other people's opinions don't matter, like, at all. As long as you have a goal to achieve, you'll be able to reach it, no matter what.

And I hope my journey through the English language has inspired you too, even a little bit.

What you need to know

As you have discovered, it hasn't been easy to master a foreign language. However, languages open doors to worlds you didn't even know existed. Here are some tips I wish I had known before learning English...

Getting the basics

In retrospect, I think primary school or high school aren't the right places to learn a language because, as a child, you don't even know if it's going to be good for you or not. You just go along, learning what adults want you to learn.

So, first and foremost, the **motivation needs to come from you**, not from someone else. I am sure that, if you have a good enough reason to learn a language, you'll be able to master it in a reasonable amount of time. You can do many things at home to help you get the basic vocabulary: watch movies and TV shows, listen to music, read novels or nonfiction...

But there are things you can't do alone. I would advise you to **find a practice group**, like a roundtable, in your area. If you're starting the language, you can also find a course that will help you get those basics quickly.

When it comes to languages, the thing is to have a goal. Once you've set a goal, you'll then find the motivation to achieve everything that comes your way.

Beyond the basics

My parents didn't get it all wrong when they sent me to the United Kingdom to learn English (don't tell them, though!) It was simply down to bad timing. So, if you have time and a budget, go for an

immersion course in an English-speaking country. Practising with natives, or people trying to learn just like you, is absolutely worth it.

I would advise you to let go of your fear of looking ridiculous when speaking a language that you haven't yet mastered. **Everyone makes grammatical mistakes**. People are usually kind enough to correct you if you have made one: they know you're learning. Also, let's face it, you also make mistakes when speaking your mother tongue. As long as you're understandable, it's all fine.

As the saying goes, "Practice makes perfect."

Last but not least, if you like the idea of **correspondence**, there are a couple of websites that help you find pen-pals from all over the world. I have had three of them over the past few years, and it was a real pleasure to talk about life with someone from Ireland, Germany or Japan.

The IELTS exam

I have devoted this section to the IELTS exam. Not only is it a difficult English certification test, but it also has its specific aspects. You can't just show up to the exam and pass it. It is definitely not a piece of cake.

Well, actually, I am sure native speakers could pass it like that, but certainly not non-natives like me who had recently started seriously learning the language. So here are my tips on how to prepare to pass it like a pro.

What is IELTS?

IELTS stands for International English Language Testing System. It's an English test for someone for whom English is not their mother tongue. You usually need to pass it if you want to live or study in an English-speaking country.

Is it a recognised test?

IELTS is internationally recognised by more than 9,000 organisations. The British government created it in 1989 for visa enquiries. Cambridge English, in collaboration with the British Council, IELTS organisation and IDP: IELTS Australia, conceived the IELTS test. So yes, this is a serious and recognised test.

How is it structured?

IELTS is divided into four parts:

1. **Listening** (30 minutes): You'll listen to an audiotape and answer 40 questions about it. The audio is divided into four parts, from the easiest to the hardest. You have time to read the questions in advance (because the instructions are included in the audio). But

you'll hear the audio only once, so listen carefully. You are marked according to your answers. A 35/40 is equal to a Band 8, a 30/40 to a Band 7, etc.

2. **Reading** (1 hour): As with the listening part, you'll answer 40 questions. The test is divided into three parts according to the difficulty of the texts, which are taken from newspapers and magazines. This is marked in the same way as the listening part.

3. **Writing** (1 hour): You'll have to write two texts. The first is a 150-word bar chart or graph description (doable in 20 minutes). The second is a 250-word essay (which should be feasible in 40 minutes). What they mark is your grammar, spelling, vocabulary and consistency, if you have succeeded in reaching the word count, whether or not you answered the question.

4. **Speaking** (15 minutes): This is divided into three parts, although they are short compared to the previous parts of the test. Firstly, you'll talk about known subjects, such as your home country, your family, your work, etc. Secondly, you'll prepare a specific question for about one minute, then talk about it for between one and two minutes. The examiner will stop you if he considers you have answered the question, or if you have overrun the time. Then he'll ask you two questions about what you have just said. Finally, you'll be asked harder questions about an endless array of subjects you're not necessarily familiar with. What they mark is your pronunciation, your grammar, your vocabulary, your way of expressing yourself (whether it seems natural or not) and if you answered the questions.

Two types of IELTS

As I said above, there are two possible reasons why you might need to pass the test. So it's only logical that there are two types of IELTS. But don't worry, the differences are minimal.

- **Academic**: This is the hardest test of the two. You do this one if you want to study at an English-speaking university. Lots of universities ask for it, to avoid students registering if they don't have a sufficient level of English. It would be a shame if you couldn't understand a word of your lectures, wouldn't it?

- **General Training**: This is the easiest option just to make sure that you're able to live in an English country without any problem. The reading should be easier to understand than in the Academic one. You'll still have to answer 40 questions in one hour, but I think it is easier to get a high score in the General Training tests. When it comes to the writing part, the bar chart or graph is replaced by a letter. You'll write a piece of correspondence between you and a friend, or you and a company, for example.

How do the bands work?

A Band categorises you according to your English level.

- **Band 9** = English is your mother tongue or close to it (C2)

- **Bands 8, 7.5 and 7** = You're an advanced speaker (C1)

- **Bands 6.5, 6 and 5.5** = You're an upper-intermediate speaker (B2)

- **Bands 5, 4.5 and 4** = You're a lower-intermediate speaker (B1)

Below those bands, well... I don't think it's necessary to pay for the exam if you're a beginner.

How can I attend the test?

In 2015 in the UK, at the time I passed it, the IELTS fee was £150. I checked recently, and it was £175, but the price might have changed. Have a look at the official IELTS website (https://takeielts.britishcouncil.org/) and book a slot. You can also choose the place, time and date you would like to pass it.

How do you prepare for IELTS?

I did a lot of preparation for the test. I took a special IELTS course which helped me prepare for all its particular features, and I can't recommend it enough. It helped me improve my writing, working on essays about any topic, and practising bar charts and graph descriptions. To be fair, it's unlikely that you'll have to do that in real life, but it's super useful if you're planning on attending a British or American university.

Test yourself with fake IELTS exams. You can find a lot of them over the internet, and even in IELTS books. Use and abuse them because you'll understand the test better, you'll get what you need to do to perform at your highest potential. In four words: you need a strategy.

Any advice, Estelle?

- **Don't forget your ID** and **be on time**, they're super rigorous.

- **Try not to panic**. I know, you have trained hard for this and don't want to mess up. That's understandable. But panicking will only slow you down and get you all over the place. Breathe, you got this!

- **Listening**: Read the questions and imagine the possible answers. Of course, listen carefully to the audiotape because you'll hear it only once. However, be careful with your spelling. If you make one mistake, they'll say it's an incorrect answer.

• **Reading**: Read and underline what's important within the questions before rushing on to the texts. It will help you to know what you're looking for and to avoid wasting time.

• **Writing**: Answer the question without going off-topic. I know it sounds complicated, but if you have trained yourself, you can absolutely do it. Analyse the chart(s) and make a little plan on paper before actually writing your description. Always reach the minimum word count because it counts for your marks. And take your time, even if you only have one hour to go.

• **Speaking**: Your examiner will record your speaking test but try to disregard that. Answer the whole question (especially the second part) because they won't hesitate to mark you down. It is time to show that you're capable of having a conversation and that you have achieved a high level of fluency.

How long before you get your results?

It will take around two weeks before you get your marks. I had to pick them up in person, but you might be able to ask for them to be sent to you via email or post.

If, by any chance, you passed the IELTS exam after reading this book, please let me know how it went by emailing me at vdvestelle.author@gmail.com. I would be delighted to know you rocked!

3. University

Following the dream

I always wanted to be an author, but never allowed myself to become one. There's always been a weird mentality about creativity in the French-speaking world. You were seen as either having a gift for writing or not. And when you had the chance to write for a living, others would always consider it as a hobby. Like you definitely had to do something else for a living because having a passion could not possibly pay, right? That wouldn't be fair for everyone else working their asses off in jobs they weren't passionate about.

I decided to go back to university and do a master's degree in creative writing. Not that I needed to learn how to write, but I did need to allocate time for it. When I had looked in Belgium or France, no such master's seemed to exist. But I found it in the UK.

When talking about my project, I was met with many clichéd questions and statements.

"Isn't it a waste of time?"

"What are the job opportunities with such a master's degree?"

"You should try finding a real job."

For a long time, I believed them. I believed I had to find a "real" job that would earn good money, and write only as a hobby. But deep down, I felt that I wasn't allowing myself to be me. I had been unemployed for more than a year, and was still unable to find a job. My parents had taught me that studies were important in life because they were the key to higher responsibilities and higher salaries. Doing a master's sounded like the right thing to do.

With the IELTS certificate in hand, I was ready to apply to the programme of my life. However, British universities didn't just need the results of an English test. They wanted me to earn my place among them.

Education systems vary from one country to another. When I did my bachelor's degree in Journalism in Belgium, at the Haute École de Louvain en Hainaut in Tournai, I didn't have to "apply" but to "enrol" on one of the university programmes. In Belgium, as long as you pay the tuition fee, you're good to go. Needless to say, the process was different in the United Kingdom.

At the same time as I was preparing for the IELTS exam, I was also preparing my applications. It wasn't something I had experienced in the past, so I didn't know what to expect. What I did know was that I had to write a cover letter for each university, stating why I wanted to enter their creative writing programme. Okay... but which universities? There were plenty of them and, to be honest, I had only heard about Cambridge and Oxford, as they are kind of world-famous.

The university I was aiming for was the Royal Holloway in Central London – the nearest tube station was Russell Square. It was closer to where I lived at the time: we had moved away from the Russian Airbnb by then and were renting our first flat in Kentish Town. The Royal Holloway seemed to have the best programme: it was really focused on writing. You could either choose to follow a fiction, non-fiction or poetry path. But every university seemed to ask for different things when applying. One would request a critique of a book, another would want to read an excerpt of your writing.

I ended up applying to four universities. As I mentioned, I read *Jonathan Strange & Mr Norrell* by Susanna Clarke, and wrote a critique. I drafted the first version of my short story, *Finding Maxwell*, which has now been self-published. And I gave an account of why I was the best fit for their programmes. I hit "send" at the beginning of

August 2015, right after receiving my IELTS results, hoping one of them would accept my application.

But I wasn't done yet. I also had to ask for two references: one private and one professional. My previous company agreed to write one, even though not a lot of people there spoke English. The trickiest part was that I couldn't ask a family member or a friend to vouch for me for the private one. And I didn't know a lot of people in the UK, as we had only been there for six months! I couldn't believe that my applications might fail for this reason.

"I will do it for you," Tessa said.

She was the coordinator of the English speaking class I was attending in parallel with the IELTS course.

"Although I have only known Estelle for a short period, I am aware of her creative writing and also critical reviews and I believe she is a very suitable candidate for the MA Creative Writing course. I am sure her existing writing talents will benefit greatly from the course and that she will be an enthusiastic and diligent student," she wrote.

I couldn't be more grateful. We just had to cross our fingers that everything would fall into place.

From the four universities, I received two unconditional offers. One, a different London university, was close to home but it had a bad ranking. As every British university is ranked on a couple of criteria, the higher the rank, the better the education and degree, or at least one would assume so. That university was a Plan B, I had applied there just in case.

The second unconditional offer came from a university on the opposite side of London. My eyes had gone wide with excitement when had I received an email from Brunel University with a request for an interview. Though I had had no idea I would have to go through a hiring process to attend university. The experience was so different to the one I was used to.

Brunel University was more than an hour's commute from the place we called home. I took the tube from Caledonian Road, changed at King's Cross and arrived in Uxbridge. My journey didn't end there: I still had to walk twenty minutes to the campus. I was wearing a blue dress that I usually wore at weddings – it had become my interview outfit over the past months.

I was sweating a lot, especially my hands, which I desperately tried to dry on the dress. It was kind of a mess, but we were in the middle of summer. There wasn't much I could do about it at this point.

It was my first time on campus, and I looked at it as if I already knew I would be studying there. I was also panicking because they had said it was an interview... What on earth did they want to interview me for? I was walking cliché of a creative writing student: introverted, shy and just wanting to be left alone.

I arrived in front of the office ten minutes early. David was the professor in charge of the master's I wanted to pursue. I was always early for an interview, even though I knew people weren't all that punctual and that I often ended up waiting for longer than I wanted to.

I knocked on the door.

The office was decorated with lots of books stacked high on the floor in a kind of messy library. David was a thin man in his fifties or sixties, you couldn't guess. And he was silver-haired! We sat there for an hour, talking about books we enjoyed and how David liked the story I had sent for my application.

"Did you find it difficult to write the story from a male point of view?" he asked.

"No, it just came to me naturally."

"Regarding your IELTS results–"

I froze. Of course, he had to talk about my results, I wasn't a native speaker after all.

"–I notice your grades on the writing test are lower than a band 7, even though you have an overall of 7.5. Do you think you can handle the master's?"

I had a 6 in writing. Would that be the end of my university adventure because of it?

"I will do everything I can," I nodded.

In the end, it didn't feel like an interview after all, more like I was meeting up with a friend after a long time apart.

When I left the office, I prayed that he would decide to accept me on the course. I didn't have any news from the Royal Holloway yet. But my heart was now split between it and Brunel. The programme looked great, with screenwriting and fiction writing, as well as a short course to get a sense of how to manage a creative career. My gut was telling me this programme was all I wanted.

The next day, I received an email from David. An unconditional offer! I accepted it right away.

Later, I would receive a rejection letter from the Royal Holloway.

No regrets...

After accepting the seat at Brunel, David sent me a list of no less than twenty-two books to read during the first semester. It included *Killing Monica* by Candace Bushnell, *Refugee Boy* by Benjamin Zephaniah – who was also teaching in my master's – and *Seize the*

Day by Saul Bellow. Students were expected to read two books per week. David was giving me a headstart. I struggled a lot during that semester because I had never read two books a week, even on my good days. We were meant to discuss the books the next week, so I had to read them.

Anyway, in September 2015, I pushed the doors of Brunel. I discovered that my group contained ten students from all different backgrounds. They were young and old, students and workers. They had come to Brunel to live their dreams and learn the craft of writing. All of these people were just like me, and it was incredible to be among them.

Our course involved big names in British literature, such as Benjamin Zephaniah, Will Self, Frazer Lee and Tony White. I also heard the name Bernardine Evaristo – who co-won the Man Booker Prize in 2019 – in the corridor, but she wasn't teaching on my programme.

I was at university for one day a week. It doesn't sound much, but it was just the tip of the iceberg. That first semester, we all had to produce two short stories per week while doing our reading. And not only did we have to write it, but we also gave and received feedback on each and every piece. I would have loved to have been more involved in Brunel's student life: joining the Writer's Society, taking Japanese courses or writing for Brunel's newspaper. But I was too busy trying to keep up with the master's, and I wasn't living on campus.

David pushed me hard so I would succeed. He encouraged me every week, giving me confidence in my writing and in finding my voice as a writer. But he didn't prepare me for the grading system.

I received my first grades in January, after handing in two assignments. The first grade was a B, and I had no idea what it meant. In Belgium, our grades are in percentages, so I googled what a B would translate to.

"60 to 69%?!" I shouted. "What the hell?"

"It's a high score," David explained. "A strong pass."

I raised an eyebrow. In Belgium, 69% means you barely passed. I guessed I had to accept that it wasn't the same thing in the United Kingdom.

The second semester was lighter than the first one in terms of assignments. But I couldn't rest on my laurels: I still had to submit my dissertation. It consisted of a 14,000-word story and a 5,000-word personal critique. The story is the beginning of a novel, called *Once Upon A Sky* – yet to be published.

I remember the stress of the last-minute rush. I had taken a paid internship at a small company based in Walthamstow, on the Victoria Line. And at the same time I was working my ass off on the dissertation, trying to meet the deadline.

"They're telling us, three days before submission day, that we have to print it!? It's all been done electronically until now," I moaned.

I took a day off and travelled to Uxbridge, where I printed the dissertation at the university's library. What a happy day – but also stressful – to come back on campus, and hand in my work!

In December 2016, I graduated with merit. I'm still not sure what it means, but all I could see was my mum's pride when I told her.

"My daughter graduated from an English university," she kept saying. "With merit!"

I learned a great deal at Brunel, and have grown a lot as a writer since then. I always find it challenging to sit down and write. And once I'm in the zone, I can't help but judge my writing harshly. My year at Brunel forced me to focus on my writing and to submit my work whether I liked it or not. I had to face the critique of others, and I have learned from it.

I spent one of the best years of my life (so far) at Brunel University. Not only was I doing what I had dreamed of doing since forever, but I was surrounded by like-minded people. Would I recommend the experience? If you have the motivation and finances to do it, then jump! It's all worth it.

What you need to know

Do you want to apply to British universities? Be aware that it is a journey. Not only do you have to prepare your case, but some universities want to see you for an interview or ask you to find people to vouch for you. I truly felt as though I was applying for a job, not for an educational opportunity. But fear not: I have got your back.

Selecting your university

Who said universities were the only ones to select their students? You also have the right to choose your university. Be aware that universities are ranked according to a number of criteria, the top universities being, of course, Cambridge and Oxford.

The higher the rank, the better the employer's consideration. Or that's how it is supposed to be. To be honest, I don't think it matters that much on your CV. It's what you do with your time – internships, volunteering, personal projects such as founding a short movie company, etc. – that counts.

However, Britons don't have a monopoly on this. Americans rank their universities too. So I would advise you to check the latest rankings from a trustworthy source. Try *The Guardian* or *Forbes*. They are usually the best you can find. You can even sort the tables by subject area, which gives you an even clearer view of which university to select according to the studies of your choosing.

Writing your covering letter

It is officially called a Personal Statement but don't be fooled: it's a covering letter. You'll have to explain to your potential future tutor that you're worthy of being on their programme and why you want to study the subject. In my case, I just poured my heart out on paper and talked about what writing meant to me. I think it did the trick.

Getting recommendations

You'll probably have to provide references: one private, one professional. The latter is the easiest to get, as long as you've previously worked somewhere, maybe a student job you did in your school years, or if you volunteered. As for the private one, you'll have to find someone who's known you for at least five years and isn't a family member – say bye-bye to your mum's recommendation – or a friend. Or, if you're lucky, someone who's known you for a few months will do.

Conditional VS Unconditional

The university can either refuse or accept your application. If it accepts it, there are two types of offers. The first is the **unconditional** offer, which means that you have got your place confirmed and you just have to accept or refuse it. The second one is the **conditional** offer, which means you still have to meet some criteria before your place is confirmed. It means they're interested in having you; you're just not fully qualified yet.

Receiving an unconditional offer isn't the end of the journey. Before accepting, make sure you understand everything it implies. If you agree, it means you're committed to going to that university. Be careful to understand what it could mean for you financially.

What's the price of my education?

Prices vary depending on whether you're British, European or from overseas. Let me give you an example:

For a master's in creative writing, you could either do it full-time or part-time. Full-time means you have to pay the tuition fee in a year. Part-time means you can take the masters in two years instead of one, and so schedule the payments accordingly.

Now, let's talk about money:

British and European students would pay £8,240 full-time, while overseas students would pay £17,355 full-time for the same master's in creative writing.

Disclaimer: with Brexit, I don't know if British and European students' tuition fees will stay the same in the future. The prices are from brunel.ac.uk, academic year 2020/21 and are subject to an annual increase.

You can try getting a scholarship to fund your education if you qualify for the conditions set by the government or the university.

What's my grades?

In the United Kingdom, you have to cope with a lot of grading systems. Whether it's for a course, a bachelor's degree or a master's degree. An A isn't the same as a first or a distinction. Make sure you understand what it means, and don't be pissed off – like me – when you discover how it translates into your country's grading system.

Here's the grading system for a **simple course**:

- A is the highest grade;

- B is a strong pass;

- C is a pass;

- Below C, I am afraid it doesn't sound good.

For a **bachelor's degree**:

- First (1st);
- Second class honours upper division (2.1);
- Second class honours lower division (2.2);
- Third (3rd);
- Fail.

For a **master's degree**:

- Distinction;
- Merit;
- Pass;
- Fail.

4. Job Hunting

Struggles can be overcome

Did you always know exactly what you wanted to do in your life? Or do you know someone who did?

My first experience in a permanent role started just after I graduated from university in Belgium, in 2011. I was an administrative assistant on paper but was doing practically everything, from organising events to managing social media. I fell victim to false rumours that denigrated my professionalism and skills, and there were only two of us permanent employees – I knew exactly who it was coming from. Two years in that role burned me out, so I quit. My confidence had been crushed: I thought I was no good to anyone and I was certainly a bit depressed.

Moving to London, I thought everything was possible. Jobs were within my reach and all I had to do was to hold on to that thought. However, I quickly understood that you have to be willing to do things you might not want to, to get your foot in the door. Or you need to have a rock-solid CV because London doesn't give you a job by clicking your fingers – unless you're a developer... hi Quentin!

In April 2015, on a Wednesday morning, I was standing in Victoria Station, in the heart of London. There were so many people in the station, getting on with their busy lives, waiting for a train or rushing into the tube. They knew what they were doing, they were confident. I was not.

My destination was an office stuck in between the McDonald's and the station's toilets. It was the office of an international coffee shop brand that had a couple of stores in London. And no, it wasn't Starbucks.

I was immediately greeted by a receptionist with a strong London accent.

"Please take a seat. Here's a form you'll have to fill in. Let me know when it's done and someone will see you."

I took a seat next to the window at the entrance to the office. First name, last name... I often mixed the two up. I hoped I hadn't made a mistake by writing my first name in the last name's box. How bad would that look? I didn't know.

I gave the form back and waited a couple of minutes before a short man came to meet me for the interview. He led me to a room a bit further from the reception. After a couple of questions, he finally asked: "would you mind doing night shifts?"

Night shifts... I thought these people were just selling sandwiches during the day, but they were apparently also making them during the night. My thoughts went to Quentin. I was already seeing so little of him because he had started a job as a developer – a day-job.

"No," I answered.

My fate was sealed: no job in a coffee shop for me. I was definitely privileged in being able to say no. I just wasn't ready.

In between April and May 2015, I sat in different buildings, different offices, filled in many forms, and answered lots of questions. But none of them seemed to be the right fit.

I once applied for a freelance translator role and had to do a test from English to French, to check if I had the right skills for the job. They told me I was making too many spelling mistakes, which I was sure I wasn't. And after asking for a proofreading document, they never answered me ever again. In the meantime, another company had told me I was overqualified for the role I had applied to. Which one do you think I believed? My confidence was crushed, once again.

Brunel University happened to have a grant programme for students who wanted to intern in a company. I applied and interviewed for a couple of internships before finding the one. Not far from Walthamstow station, at the end of the Victoria Line, I entered the world of a small ecommerce company as a digital marketing assistant for three months, from mid-July to mid-October 2016.

It was a full-time paid internship. The grant provided half of the salary and the ecommerce provided the other half. The job gave me the foot in the door I needed to get back into the business world. I learned a few new concepts, such as SEO (Search Engine Optimisation) and how to work out an ecommerce website in multiple languages, both of which would be key for the future of my career.

I thought this internship would be the beginning of my luck, especially since the owner – a tall French woman in her fifties – offered to continue working with her after the internship... only as a freelancer. It was August 2016, Quentin and I had moved to Brighton (more on that in the next chapter), and being freelance sounded like a great opportunity.

"Grow your client base, and you'll be fine," the owner told me.

Yes, in theory!

I wasn't dripping in confidence. More than that: I have never been the kind of person able to sell themselves and attract clients. The money I was making working for the ecommerce company was enough to pay for my part of the rent, but nothing else. But I had savings, and Quentin kindly kept telling me I should take the time to write my book.

So I started to write. It was a book called *Once Upon A Sky*, a young adult fantasy novel which I'm still writing at this point and that I already mentioned in this book.

I got into the habit of going to the local library every morning, to do my one-hour writing session, then coming back home never to leave the flat again that day. I was craving human contact, though. I found being alone in the flat all day long a terrible thing.

I had an interview at my favourite bookshop in Brighton in October 2016, and was rejected a couple of days later. I cried for hours on my own, while Quentin was at work. Thoughts of uselessness crossed my mind a few times; I wasn't even able to land a job like that... I ended up crying for a week before I was finally able to get my act together.

"When will you finally get a job? Are you even looking?" asked a very dear family member.

I dropped off covering letters and CVs into pretty much every shop in Brighton that day. I was so angry that everyone was always asking me the same question, so fed up with everything and everyone that I simply applied everywhere I could.

A big supermarket chain was the first to answer my plea. Wearing my interview dress, I took the bus to the leading shop in Kingston by Sea, approximately 30 minutes from where we lived. Unsurprisingly, I wasn't the only one applying and being interviewed. They said they would call in the lucky ones: I didn't get that call.

A couple of days later, I went to a tea company's warehouse for an unpaid test – filling bags with tea and labelling them for a couple of hours. I did receive two bags of tea for my service, but hadn't been quick enough. I think my attention to detail didn't help. I had been taught by my pharmacist parents to weigh things perfectly, give or take a few grams.

It was starting to seem like moving to Brighton hadn't been the brightest idea. Quentin had kept his London job: they had agreed to let him work from home three days a week. But a change of manager had made commuting every day mandatory once again. The money spent on train fares was huge (beware of them!), but he was also becoming increasingly exhausted. I could see he had no energy left for his own projects – he's a musician in his spare time. I tried to make his life as easy as possible, by making dinner so it would be ready as soon as he got home for example, but you could see the fatigue on his face.

"Should we move back to London, or stay and make it work here in Brighton?" Quentin asked one day, after we had come back from visiting our family in Belgium.

By April 2017, I had unfortunately heard that question increasingly often, which made me doubt even more of my choices.

A recruiter called me with a dream job, or what seemed to be one. It was a marketing role within a second-hand book retailer. I had always wanted to work in the book industry, so I applied. The position sounded a little out of my comfort zone, but I gave everything I had at the first interview. Even better: the interviewer was French and kind of wanted to hire someone like me!

There was a dilemma though. The job was close to Brighton, and we were talking about potentially moving back to London. I couldn't find anything to stop the depression knocking on my door. I finally had a job that could be mine if I wanted it, but a little voice in my head was telling me I couldn't have it because we were about to move again.

Out of spite for myself, I dumped the opportunity. I think it was the hardest thing I had ever done because I wanted a job so badly at this point. But I knew it wasn't going to be the right job for me, as it was so far away from London.

There were two problems with my non-employment situation. The first was the city: I couldn't find anything in Brighton or near Brighton. Or maybe I just didn't try hard enough. The second was I didn't even know where we would be living in the next month. Quentin and I were thinking of moving, but we couldn't agree on where. Amsterdam, Berlin, Paris, London, Brussels... If I was going to hunt for a job, I needed to know where to look.

Okay, there was also a third problem: I couldn't get my head around what it was I truly wanted to do. I had graduated from public relations and journalism, but also creative writing. My experience was in doing nothing and everything, and I had no idea what I wanted to do with my life.

Writing fiction full-time wasn't a solution, I couldn't allow myself to do just that. While I had finished writing the first draft of *Once Upon A Sky*, the novel I had started months before, I needed to be earning a living to feel good about myself. Even though I now know that being an author is an achievable goal, I wasn't considering it at all at that stage.

I cried a lot. I was completely and utterly lost.

I had reached rock bottom. The only way was up, right?

Natasha, a brown-haired recruiter from Brighton, held a conference at a local event organised by the Brighton Digital Women in May 2017, which I attended. She talked about the importance of having a well-made, attractive CV. And it opened my eyes: I had been doing it all wrong! With her help, I completely revamped it, and I applied to as many interesting jobs as I could.

And it worked!

I landed two interviews in a very short amount of time: one in Brighton, one in London.

The first company was a start-up in the education industry based in Brighton, next to the train station. They were looking for someone who was specialised in paid search, who would be able to write ads on Google and optimise them. I wasn't a specialist so I don't know how I did it, but I passed the first interview. I learnt everything on the go while I was doing the assignment, as I felt I didn't have the correct level of skills to be hired. At the second interview, I met the team and their final conclusion was that I was too junior.

The second company was based in London, between Chancery Lane and Farringdon. They were looking for a French SEO content writer. Again, I knew very little about Search Engine Optimisation, the art of optimising a web page for Google in order for the web page to be ranked higher in the search results. But I knew I could handle the writing. I went to the first interview feeling that I had nothing to lose. I met with Richard, the SEO manager, a kind-hearted man in his early thirties, in the reception area. He brought me into a tiny room on the same floor. It was just the two of us.

"Do you like writing?" he said.

"I love writing, you mean. I'm an author – I've published a short story back in March – and I also have a blog in English."

"Yes, I read it. Impressive."

Weirdly enough, I was calm and smiling during the interview. Nothing to do with the real, stressed version of myself. It made a good first impression. Richard seemed so happy having met me that he showed me the whole office after our discussion. It was on two floors in a very tall building. They had a huge, colourful lunch area with the option to play ping pong.

I reached the second stage of the hiring process, and I wasn't surprised. I had a smile from ear to ear but I didn't want to jinx it.

There was an assignment to work on.

It involved a piece of writing. SEO optimised, of course. Marie-Hélène, my friend from Belgium was (and still is) an expert in online marketing: she helped me a great deal with it. Two days later, I submitted the assignment and I was invited for a second interview straight away.

I met Richard again, in early July 2017. My palms were damp this time, because I knew they were likely to ask me specific SEO questions and I wasn't sure I would be able to answer them. In the room were three people: Alexandra, the Spanish SEO writer, Nicole, the social media manager and Richard, of course. Their eyes were on me all the time, examining me and the answers I produced.

The interview ended and that was it. They left the room poker-faced without saying goodbye, no smiles at all.

My gut was telling me that I had failed. I was ready to send out new CVs and covering letters.

Three days later, they emailed me to arrange a call for the next day. I was upset: why wouldn't they tell me right away if it was a yes or a no? I needed a straightforward answer to understand what's going on, I don't like it when people beat around the bush. Quentin, however, was enthusiastic and hopeful. Why would they want to call me if it was to reject me? But I had had so many rejections over the previous months that I couldn't believe I would succeed.

Richard offered me the job the next day. After months of hunting and research and training, I had landed my first permanent role in the UK! I was over the moon. Quentin and I celebrated it in a pub near our Brighton flat, where we had the best burger and chips ever. We moved back to London in early August 2017, around the same time as I started at the company.

My time there was terrific.

In November 2017, after I had only been there three months, I was sent to France as a travel writer trying out train journeys. I went to Paris, Marseille, Montpellier, Lyon, Bordeaux... in just a week – and I had just gotten married the week before! I also visited Cambridge. I couldn't dream of a better job.

After nine months, I had been promoted to senior SEO content writer and was managing a team of two people. It made me grow so much as a person and as a professional.

I worked there for nearly two years. In a way, it broke my heart when I decided to leave because this was the first job that had ever made me feel good about myself. It was the first one where things were organised, where people told me I was doing great, and where I felt valued.

Why did I leave? I'll explain soon.

What you need to know

Getting a job – especially your first – is always scary. Sending a CV and a covering letter is easy compared to being interviewed. I know I get highly stressed during interviews because I never know how to sell myself and my skills. However, as I did eventually manage to get my foot in the door of some companies during my time in London, I do have some tips for you.

Getting a rock-solid CV

CVs are subjective. Everyone has an opinion on what they should or shouldn't look like. I had written many CVs over the years, and I was still struggling. However, there are things you definitely need to have on your curriculum vitae:

• **Contact details**. Don't make the error of not putting your first name, your surname, your phone number and email address. Recruiters must know right away who you are and how they can contact you if your CV matches their expectations. However, you can drop the picture. Although it's a must-have on a French CV, it's not necessary (and often unwelcome) on a British one.

• **Personal statement**. The personal statement is one or two lines after your contact details that will explain what you would like to achieve in your career and where you're coming from.

• **Skills and tools**. If you're fluent in a couple of languages, or if you have skills in particular software, that's typically the type of thing you want to add in this category. I would suggest you skim the job offer, looking for the tools used, and write them down on your CV if you think you know how to use them.

• **Professional experience**. What if your CV was a story? What kind of story would you tell? I imagine you would like one in which you would be the hero, right? That's pretty much what you need to do: write down your experience to put yourself in the best position possible. Don't forget to explain what the company was about, in which industry (retail, tech, travel, B2B, B2C, etc.) because it will help the recruiters to match your profile with the job description. Also, a tip I received from Natasha, the recruiter I mentioned earlier in my story, is that you should group all the roles you have had in one company. It is a sign that you have been growing within a company and that your managers trusted you. And don't forget to talk about your achievements in all your roles to date.

• **Education, training and other qualifications**. You don't need to be as specific as you are with your professional experience. A simple list of dates, universities and courses will do the trick. And if you have any holes in your experience, don't forget to fill them in during this section.

• **Interests and hobbies**. You may think this is a category that employers overlook, but it's not. This is your chance to be a little bit creative. Reading, for example, is a widespread hobby. It's been put on so many CVs that recruiters are not impressed any more. But if you add the kind of authors you read and why you like them, it might up your game. It's a category that helps people get to know you outside of work, so don't neglect it.

And, of course, make sure that everything is free of spelling and grammatical mistakes.

Writing a killer covering letter

A covering letter's purpose is to complement your CV with a personal human touch. It is the first impression you're going to make on your potential employer. Why do you want to work for the company you're applying to? Why should they hire you instead of George, who may have better qualifications? Be confident; you've got this...

Here are some tips:

- Be 100% sure there are **no typos** in there.

- **Make the letter about the job**, not about you. You'll be able to talk about you at the interview. But first, you need to convince the recruiter that you'll be an excellent fit for the role they're advertising.

- If you're applying via email, your covering letter should be the **body of the email.** It doesn't make sense to send an email with a covering letter and CV attached if it's to say the same thing in the email and in the attached letter.

- **Tell a story**. Covering letters can be boring. But if you're telling a compelling story, the recruiter will notice you.

- There are many templates out there. But be careful **not to send a generic letter**, though. Nobody wants to read the same text 100 times. It's likely to go in the bin.

- Be sure to **name the recruiter and the company** in the letter. An unpersonalised email only shows one thing: you haven't done any research. Why would they bother with you if you didn't bother with them in the first place?

How to nail an interview

You've got it! You have impressed the recruiter with your killer CV and covering letter. Now it's time to meet them in real life. Here's your chance to shine, so try not to panic.

I am not an expert in interviews. I can only talk about my own experience, and I often struggle myself. But here are my top tips:

• Make absolutely sure **you know enough about the company**. If you're in marketing, know about the latest news and competitors. If you're a developer, know which language they use. If you're a designer, have a look at their graphic charts... You get the idea.

• **Dress accordingly**. You don't want to show yourself in a Hawaiian shirt while your interlocutor is wearing a suit, do you? But it can also go the opposite way: why wear a suit when everyone is dressed in casual clothes?

• **Prepare for all the possible questions you might face**. If you're a non-native speaker, have a look at some standard interview questions and prepare a couple of answers. This way, you won't be taken by surprise, and you'll impress the recruiter by how fluent and prepared you are.

• **Ask questions**. At the end of the interview, the recruiter will check if you have any questions about the role and the company. Make sure you prepare some questions to ask before leaving. It shows your interest.

Freelancing in the UK

If you're done with being permanent within a company, you can easily set yourself up as a freelancer. As long as you don't earn more than a certain amount of money per year (the threshold was around £11,000 in 2016 when I did it), you're tax-free. You only pay taxes on the money you earn above that threshold, which is quite reasonable.

You will need to create a business account with the HM Revenue and Customs (or HMRC for short) and tell them you're a freelancer. You'll need your National Insurance Number, so make sure you have it.

Be careful as, if you're a permanent employee in a company but have previously set yourself as a freelancer, your taxes will be higher than they should be. In that case, either you can stop your period of freelance work by calling the HMRC, or you prolong it because it's financially worth it overall.

5. Housing

Home is where the heart is

Finding a home isn't difficult in London. We saw a ton of beautiful flats and duplexes on Rightmove – a website you'll definitely use a lot if you're looking for a new place. The problems are more about questions like "where should we start?" and "are we quick enough?" London is huge and the housing market moves fast. Every single day, people are looking for a place to live.

But let's rewind a little bit: soon after Quentin and I had moved to the UK, we were in our second Airbnb and Quentin landed his first permanent role in London. This was in April 2015. You can imagine that we were craving our own place – so we would be a young couple moving in together in their first real flat.

If you don't know the city, I'd advise you to consult a map of London at this point in the story.

The first flat we visited was part of a Victorian building with a porch surrounded by white pillars in South Kensington. It seemed like the typical British house I'd been dreaming about, watching the movie of *Pride and Prejudice*. We met with the estate agent – let's call him Garry – at the entrance of the building.

"Ready to see the place? I'm sure it'll suit you, it's a very nice flat. The area is quite lovely as well," he said.

The property was nothing like I had imagined from the outside. The corridor leading to the flat was dark and carpeted on every step of the staircase. We set foot in the flat itself: four rooms, with carpet in the living room and the bedroom. The rent was £1,500 a month though, and neither Quentin nor I had set up a budget. We had not talked about a price range or anything before meeting with the estate agent and visiting the flat, which is stupid now that I think of it.

"Okay, we'll take it," we said.

The flat was clean, modern, and sunlit. It wasn't far from the tube station and the area was indeed rather nice. The price was a bit high, but we could afford it if both of us had a job – however, only Quentin had a job at that point.

Garry shook our hands. "Brilliant. Come to my office tomorrow to sign the paperwork, and the flat is yours."

We were both grinning: we would finally be renting our very first flat together. Adios to the small Airbnb room!

We went to the agency the next day. It was the tiniest I had ever seen. Not that I had seen a lot of them, but I was expecting something much bigger. Garry was seemingly working alone: there were only two desks and a lot of boxes on the floor, which made the place feel messy.

"Did you bring the deposit?" he asked.

Quentin and I looked at each other in confusion.

"The deposit?" I said with a little voice.

"Yes, before we sign any contract, you should pay the deposit in full to secure the property," Garry explained. "Preferably in cash."

As we walked away from the office, purportedly to the bank to get the cash, we thought it was a little dodgy. We hadn't dealt with such a significant amount of money in cash before – would our bank even be okay with us withdrawing £1,000? We didn't think so – so instead we bailed on him.

But we weren't in a hurry: we wanted to find the right place in the right area. The fact was that we hadn't explored a lot of London, and we wanted to make sure we weren't making a mistake. In my mind, we might be settling down somewhere for many years. I had only lived in two houses in more than twenty years, so I wanted a house where I'd feel at home in the long term.

Caledonian Road, North London, zone 2

After that first experience, we became a bit more careful. Quentin had started working, so I was the one in charge of going places. I finally found a lovely furnished flat between Caledonian Road and Kentish Town, in the borough of Islington. It had one bedroom with a separate kitchen, a living room and a bathroom. It also had enough space to store Quentin's new folding bike, and there was carpet in the hallway and bedroom.

The flat was in a residential area and the nearest grocery store was about twenty minutes on foot. Camden Town and Regent's Park were only a bit further down the road. We had negotiated to get a reduced rent, on condition that we would stay for two years. And we got it!

We moved in at the end of April 2015, which was incredible considering our "three-month trial" wasn't even over. And we were to have so many memories in that flat.

At the start, we camped in our living room because our mattress hadn't yet arrived. And when it did, it was too small for the bed frame! The delivery men were super nice though, because they allowed us to keep the mattress while they got us one the right size.

It was after we settled in Islington that I decided to pass the IELTS exam and do a master's in creative writing. I wrote many short stories in that flat, including *Volte-Face* – which you may have read if you're subscribed to my newsletter. My inspiration for that particular story came from a neighbour of ours, a crazy lady who would scream at all times of the day or night. She would shout and yell hysterically at 3 am... She may well have woken the whole building. It certainly kept Quentin awake though I apparently usually kept sleeping like a baby.

One of our most vivid memories is from just after our first Christmas. We carried the used tree all the way to the waste nearby centre, leaving the flat for just fifteen minutes. When we came back, there were police cars and blue stripes all over the street.

"Excuse me, we live here," we said, trying to enter our building.

"Okay, but stay home until further notice," a policeman replied.

Glancing out the window, we finally figured out there had been a fight. Someone had been stabbed and killed right in front of our flat!

The police knocked on our door to ask if we had seen something. But we hadn't been at home: that fifteen minutes had been enough time for someone to get killed!

It was a scary thought.

After a year in Islington, we decided to move. It wasn't because of the crazy lady or the fight, it was because of health issues. Our place there wasn't what you would call "new" one. The carpet was old and dusty, the humidity wasn't going anywhere but inside and it felt rather small for the two of us. We knew we had a two-year contract, but we couldn't stay any longer.

One night in May 2016, I was walking back to the house from a meetup event in Southwark, South London. Lights were flashing in the street and I realised there was an ambulance in front of our building.

"It must be for our neighbours," I thought.

I climbed up the stairs. The ambulance people were on our floor... but not for our neighbours. I saw the door open: a doctor was examining Quentin, he had a blood pressure monitor around his arm. My heart started racing and I ran in to him.

"No need to worry," he said.

Easier said than done. In fact, he had called the ambulance himself because he wasn't feeling well. Panic attacks, chest pain, breathing issues: together these had made him concerned. The humidity in the flat and the carpet – there was mould on our bedroom walls! – had made it difficult for Quentin to live comfortably in our own place. He sounded okay when he answered me though.

"I'm almost asthmatic," he announced the next day, after seeing a GP (stands for General Practitioner, therefore a doctor).

I called a professional carpet cleaning service, and I was already opening the windows all day long. But nothing worked.

So we realised we had to move. But where to?

Hove, Brighton, South of England

In spite of some reservations, we decided to move out of London in September 2016 – I had finished my master's by then and was waiting for graduation. We wanted to see the countryside, rather than living in one city without ever travelling. And we chose Brighton – or, more specifically, Hove.

Why Brighton? Because it was near the sea and just an hour from London. The air was better for Quentin's lungs, which were damaged by the polluted air of the Big Smoke as well as our mouldy Islington flat.

Were we crazy? Yes, maybe a little. After all, the train fares were crazy! We learned that lesson the hard way, as Quentin was still working in London and had to commute regularly. But we had visited so many flats in the capital and were struggling to find one without a carpet. I don't know why the British love their carpets so much. They attract dust and dirt, and they are difficult to clean... I felt like every single flat in the UK has carpets; and at that stage it was making me despair.

According to British people, they tend to choose carpets over other floorings because it's a rather cold country in winter and carpet keeps the room warm. As they live in flats, it's also quieter to walk around on carpeted floors rather than wooden ones. Still, I can't understand them.

Our flat in Brighton had a carpet, yes (unfortunately), but only in the bedroom. It was a newly renovated, unfurnished flat on the second floor of a house near Hove's train station and a cute little shopping street. The seafront was only a ten-minute walk away. And we were so much calmer and happier there.

Brighton was nothing like London. People talked to each other! I never knew my neighbours in London, whereas now I often talked with Dusty, who lived on the floor below us. It was common to be stopped by a passer-by while I was walking along the sea wall. People were taking the time to live their best life, they weren't chasing it. And so, even though I had a tough time – battling against impostor syndrome and feeling I was useless job-wise – it felt like home in Brighton. There's nothing better than feeling the fresh air filling your lungs and admiring the sunset.

My mum was so upset though!

"You're making a mistake," she muttered.

In her defence, she had visited us during a huge train strike – November 2016 was a mess. The journey from London to Brighton hadn't been smooth at all, so we couldn't blame her.

After a year in Brighton, I found a job in London. It made no sense to continue living so far away from the capital, with two jobs there. So we moved back to London in August 2017.

We visited quite a few flats within the same week. Well... I visited a few flats, because Quentin was working and we needed a new place as soon as possible.

Woodside Park, North London, zone 4

I visited one of the biggest flats I had ever seen near Woodside Park: huge ceilings, no carpets(!), two bathrooms and a big living room. I called Quentin – it was an emergency!

"Have you seen the pictures yet?" I said.

"Yes, looks amazing!" he answered.

"I'm calling the agency straight away. How about the rent?"

"Go, go, go!"

Have I mentioned that you've got to be quick in London? By the time I called the agency to secure the flat, someone else had already paid a deposit. We were upset and discouraged. I had visited so many flats already, and none of them had been good enough for us.

Two days later though, I made a bold move. I secured a flat in the same area without first agreeing it with Quentin. It had two bedrooms, no carpet and an open kitchen. The flat was bright and lovely, certainly seemed a good choice. But then...

My mind was toying with me. It was telling me the flat was tiny in comparison to our Brighton one.

"I've made a huge mistake! What if it's too small?" I said.

What if we were unable to fit in all our furniture? What if we were moving to the equivalent of a hamster's cage?

And if that wasn't enough, I was going to Paris to meet with my new job's French team so Quentin would be doing all the moving alone.

He saw the flat for the first time on the moving day. That wasn't ideal but, fortunately, he loved it. We lived there for two years, as we were getting tired of changing places each year. It was our third and last flat in the UK before we returned back to Belgium.

But that, my dear reader, is another story.

Now that I have lived in a couple of places, I can say it doesn't matter where you live. What matters is who you live with. I could live anywhere, as long as it was with Quentin by my side. I know it sounds like a cliché, but it's nonetheless true.

What you need to know

Finding a place to live is one of the biggest decisions you'll make. Will you rent a flat on your own, or will you share a home with other people? Do you want to be central or a bit further out, maybe even outside London? Or will you live in a completely different city? What are the things to look at before saying yes to a flat? And how do you inform the necessary authorities that you just moved? As usual, I've got you covered.

Looking for a flat

London is formed of the City of London – which is the original city – and 32 boroughs. The most famous boroughs are also the most expensive ones. We personally lived in Islington and High Barnet, which are both located in the north of the city.

My advice? Get a feel for the area. Travel around, check which borough attracts you the most. Once you've found where you'd like to live, go check rightmove.co.uk It's easier to visit properties in the same area than looking everywhere and doing the splits in-between visits because you have no idea where to look. Save your energy for something else, like playing the tourist.

The housing checklist

Before moving into a new place, here are some tips:

> • **Know your budget**. You can find relatively cheap and expensive places to rent in London. Work out how much you're willing to pay according to your monthly income. Don't agree to a costly rent if you're not ready to spend that much money.

- **The rent doesn't necessarily cover the charges**. In your calculation, don't forget to add an average for the services (water, electricity, gas and internet) or you'll have a nasty surprise after a couple of months. There's also something called the council tax, which is a monthly payment to your local Borough council. This is between £100 and £150 on average.

- **Check public transport**. You can end up paying a lot more for a train ticket than you need to if you don't pay attention, so make sure you check how you get from the property to the office before paying any deposit.

- **Know what you want from a place**. Do you want to live near a park, a supermarket, a shopping centre? Put a checklist together and make your choice according to whether the place ticks enough boxes. But be ready to make compromises.

- **Make a list of questions for each place you visit**. How much is the council tax? How much will the electricity be on average? Is the place well insulated? Etc.

And when you've got eyes on a property, you can expect to be asked to pay a deposit. It works like a guarantee if you damage the flat. It is supposed to be secured on a special bank account, created on the occasion with a third-party scheme. But some landlords abuse this – you have the right to check they are doing it properly. Usually, the estate agent will ask you to make an online payment.

Be wary though: some landlords see the deposit as being rightfully theirs and will use any excuse to hang on to it at the end of the tenancy.

How do I tell my country of origin that I moved?

This question is easy to answer: go to your embassy. The website will tell you what they need you to bring, so make sure you visit it. Once you're at the embassy, show the papers they need, and they'll do the work for you.

In our case, we had to show our ID cards and proof of address. The proof of address can be either an electricity or water bill, or the council tax bill with your name on it. The rental contract doesn't count, I am afraid. They will then ask you to send a letter to your local town hall in your country of origin, stating that you have moved.

And that's pretty much it. Easy, isn't it?

Moving before the end of the tenancy

Just a note on that: you'll have to pay for a fee if you break your tenancy contract before its end. When Quentin and I moved to Brighton, I've already mentioned that we were actually supposed to stay in Islington for two years. As we only stayed a year, we had to pay roughly £600 to be free from the flat... and even that was on condition that the agency could find other tenants. We were lucky that the housing market in London moves fast, otherwise we would have had to pay the rent during the empty months. So think about that before you break a contract.

How do you move places?

- Pick a **moving van** (or removals) service. There are plenty of removal services in London, which is handy if you've got a lot of things to carry around or if you're moving to another city just like we did.

• Arrange a **professional cleaning**. Some flat owners make it a condition for leaving: you've got to get the place cleaned by a professional service. Once again, just check online. I'm sure you'll be able to find one in your area.

6. Life

What it means to be Londoners

Once you've settled, you've got to live your best life. Don't make it all about work. London has so many things to offer it would be a shame not to take advantage of being in one of the busiest cities on the planet.

Culture shock? What culture shock?

Coming from Belgium, the UK isn't that different in many ways. Both are European countries, both have the same kind of weather. The big difference is that they speak English, whereas I'm a French native speaker.

"It's pronounced 'Leiter' not 'Leicester'," a friend joked one day. "'Edimbra', not 'Edinburg'."

God, why? Why do they spell a word with so many letters only to pronounce half of them? It's so incomprehensible.

On the topic of British food, I had some fun experiences. Pizza with salad on top, for example, or shepherd's pie, which isn't a pie as I would understand it. Also, why are the British so fond of having crisps right before their lunch? So weird.

But London is so cosmopolitan that the shock wasn't as big as it could have been.

British people aren't as cold as they let you think they are. They have a great sense of humour – even though I never quite understood it... However, Quentin enjoyed it so much I believe him – and they also love going to the pub to relax after work, which I wasn't used to before.

Oh! And they don't kiss to greet people. No one did, really, not even expats.

I was completely lost the first time I met Quentin's friend, Greg, a Russian black-haired guy he used to work with. In Belgium, you kiss someone on the cheek once, whether you know the person or not. So I froze: how did he like to be greeted? Would I be making a mistake if I kissed him on the cheek?

I ended up doing nothing.

Greg, if you're reading this book, now you know why I was so weird the first time we met...

Anyway, people usually prefer hugs rather than kisses on the cheek. If they are good friends, of course. Don't hug your boss or a total stranger, it would be super weird for both of you.

Relationships can either thrive or fade away

There's a French expression saying "far from the eye, far from the heart". It means that once someone moves away, nobody thinks about them anymore. Britons have a contrasting expression: "Absence makes the heart grow fonder." I personally prefer the latter – it's much more positive. However, I do believe that you truly see relationships for what they are once you live far away from each other.

"We'll visit you, for sure!" said approximately every single person we knew.

A lot of people, both friends and family members, told us they'd come over and visit us. At first, we were excited. We were planning to take them in, happy to show them where we lived, where we worked, where we went out and so on. But they never came. After a while, each time we saw them in Belgium, we would simply nod at their promises, knowing it would never happen.

I already mentioned that London is only two hours away from Belgium by train. However, for most people, it's the far end of the world.

When we were saying goodbye to everyone before taking the leap, I felt like it was the end of something. A couple of months later, I found out that one of my oldest friends had got married without telling me because they thought I wouldn't be able to make it, so they didn't even bother inviting us. It broke my heart into a thousand pieces, but I understood deep down that maybe our relationship hadn't been meant to last.

But hey, I'm not saying all relationships are doomed because you move to another country.

"I miss you," my grandad said.

I was visiting him for the first time since the move. He was on the verge of crying when he said it. Believe me, it wasn't easy to make my grandad cry.

On the other hand, my mum, who I am close to, never said she missed me. She often joked that I was the daughter she had the most contact with, even though my sisters were both still living in Belgium.

That's when I understood the extent of the impact of being an expat: you can't be at every birthday, wedding or gathering. But you can still think about your family and friends, talk to them every day and be there when it truly matters.

Making new friends

"Okay, Estelle, but how about making new friends?" you may ask.

Well, that's a bit tricky. I often hear people complain that it's hard to make new friends. At a certain point in life, people are so busy with their lives that they don't bother making new acquaintances.

When I started in London, I didn't know anybody. Except for Quentin, of course. I was so lucky to have him!

So, what do you do when you want to meet new people but are shy as hell? You go meet your boyfriend's friends, of course.

I remember going to one of Quentin's friend's birthdays. We had met him and his new girlfriend earlier when we went to see a photographic exhibition in Central London, at the Photographer's Gallery in Soho. I didn't know what I would say because I didn't know them. What if they thought I was stupid?

So I kept my mouth shut for most of the day, just listening to what they were talking about. And then, the birthday dinner came by. I was sitting in front of the new girlfriend who, I found out, didn't know anybody either. She was a student at the London School of Economics (LSE). We started talking... and it was like we had known each other forever!

That's how Justyna came into our lives. She's one of the kindest people on Earth! She's always smiling, and has always a kind word for everyone. She is from Lithuania, and loves travelling. She's been to so many countries already that I wonder which ones are left for her to discover. She has become one of my best friends, even though I eventually moved back to Belgium and she stayed in London.

I also went to a couple of writing meetups – you know my love of writing by now. I just wanted to find people who shared the same interests. Rebecca, a freelance editor and author coach, organised one event that I found particularly interesting. As someone who's super shy when meeting new people, I just had to sit down and listen to the short lecture. What I was dreading, however, was the ten minutes before the speech because we had to introduce ourselves...

"I'm Estelle, student in creative writing at Brunel University. I'm here because I love writing."

"Welcome, Estelle."

I always thought it sounded like an Alcoholics Anonymous meeting.

At one of these meetings, I met John, a London-based indie author in his fifties. We became friends and writing buddies. He is, without a doubt, one of the most interesting people I know. He knows so many things on so many topics, like a walking encyclopaedia. His kindness helped me a great deal when I was struggling with my job hunting, when I had to fill in my first UK tax return and when I was looking for a place to stay. I am glad to say we're still friends even though we don't live in the same city any more.

People say it's difficult to meet other people these days, and it's true. If it wasn't for this meetup group, I don't think I would have met John. That's why you need to get out there!

Volunteering gives you a purpose

To meet other people, but also to improve my English skills, I volunteered for almost a year at the Ministry of Stories, in Hackney. This is a charity that offers writing workshops to children in the area. They also had a small shop called High Street Monster Supplies, which is a special sweet shop. Once someone enters it, your role is to tell stories about the many things that the shop offers. As a storyteller, that was the perfect place for me to be. Not only did I learn about how to manage a shop, but I also improved my English a great deal.

Six months in, I was more confident and knew a couple of other volunteers. Emily, the shop owner, helped me out with my university applications. André, whose shift was usually at the same time as mine, had his birthday on the same day as me and was the best cupcake baker in the world. I remember the delicious days when he brought some of his baked delights to the shop for us.

After a while, I became a story mentor. I visited a local school and helped children write their school play. Of course, it was scary at first. Being surrounded by native speakers that age is somewhat terrifying because I was scared of making any mistakes that would be mocked. But it was so rewarding: seeing their motivation and happiness when we came to their class and worked on their project was all I needed to move forward.

My most vivid memory of that experience was when a boy came over to me after the session and told me a couple of words in perfect French because he wanted to let me know I was doing okay as a mentor. His mum was a French speaker and had taught him the language when he was little. I was so surprised that I couldn't say a word. But I was thankful to him because it helped me become more comfortable teaching and helping the kids, knowing they weren't that different from me.

I will forever be grateful to the Ministry of Stories for taking me in. I can't recommend volunteering enough if you feel alone in a new city, because you will meet people and gain a sense of purpose. It definitely helped me.

Happiness is just around the corner

There's one memory I will always cherish about our first flat in Islington.

It was my 28th birthday (August 2016); I had come back home from my internship at the little ecommerce in Walthamstow. Quentin was already there: I could smell the delicious fragrance from the pasta carbonara he was cooking. I had received a huge bouquet from my colleagues and some great gifts from my family. At some point in the evening, I was sitting at my desk in the living room, and Quentin walked in as he would usually do. Except that he was now kneeling in front of me.

"What are you doing?" I exclaimed.

"You know, there will never be a good time for this," Quentin said.

Tears stung my eyes. I knew what he was about to ask.

"Will you be more than just my girlfriend?"

"Yes!" And I cried my eyes out from joy. I know it sounds clichéd, but it's just like in the movies. My heart was racing, and I couldn't help but think "Is it really happening?" I couldn't believe my eyes or my ears for that matter. And when he took the engagement ring out of his pocket... Oh my god, such happiness!

What you need to know

So... meeting new people is difficult, we all know it. I have talked a lot about this with other expats and they all discuss the same question: how do you meet people? How do you make time to get to know someone?

But also, how do you make time to maintain a relationship from afar?

London offers a huge pot of opportunities for culture and work. But everyday life is so busy that people don't take the time any more. Everything has to be quick and easy.

Relationships, however, aren't fast and simple. Here are some tips to help you develop the social life of a Londoner...

Get into meetup groups

Did you know there are thousands of meetup groups? There's certainly one for you, so go ahead and participate! I met my writing buddy, John, in one of these meetings. That was the best decision I made, and I have met so many people thanks to it. So if a shy person like me could make it, you can certainly do it too.

Just go on meetup.com, select your area and choose your interests. You will then have a list of groups that already exist. There are a variety of groups, from sports and careers to languages and arts. If they organise a meetup, you will know where and when it will be held.

Get digital

If meeting up with people is too hard for you, you may want to try social media. When I first set foot in London, I had an expat and bookish blog. It helped me get acquainted with the expat and book community, and I met them in real life afterwards. Talking to people before meeting them in person really helped me out at times. It's easier to talk to someone when you have already been in contact online. However, be careful about the people you choose to meet in real life. Be sure you are safe before making the step. Always meet in a public space first.

Going digital can also help you stay in touch with your friends and family. I had, for example, started emailing my best friend once every month, telling him bits and bobs of my life. I had set up a weekly call with my mum so we could see each other via camera. It wasn't always enough but at least we were often talking to each other. With my sisters, on the other hand, we had set up a Facebook group that we still use now that I am back.

Did you say letters are old school?

The first year in London felt pretty lonely. To solve the loneliness, I subscribed to a French forum (livraddict.com) that was offering to pair people with someone in a pen pal system. I will always be grateful to Deborah and Anaelle, who I made friends with this way when I was feeling isolated. I still have tons of letters and postcards from that time, and I will always cherish them.

There's also another type of correspondence that I will always keep in my heart. My grandpa, the one who used to call us "the Londoners", wasn't on social media or the internet in general. He was from the generation that had missed out on the advances in technology. So we would send each other letters.

I can't tell you how amazing it felt to receive those letters. We're so used to instant messaging that we forget how thrilling it is to wait for an answer, and how great it is to use pen and paper to write until your hand aches. I definitely recommend the old school way if you have the time and energy to do it.

Here is a small list of websites that offer pen pal systems:

- http://www.penpalworld.com/
- https://www.conversationexchange.com/
- https://www.postcrossing.com/

On living together

"Dating someone or living with someone isn't the same thing," warned my mum. "Be careful, it might just mean the end."

I had been dating Quentin for four years before we decided to move to London. We had never lived together, but we sure were madly in love. I heard my mum's warning but dismissed it right away. And fortunately, in the end, it was just a mum's concern.

Quentin and I have similar characters so it was easy to live together. But, of course, this doesn't apply to everyone.

We are lovers, but we're also a team. When emigrating together with someone, you want to make sure you'll always support each other, have each other's back. I was lucky enough to have Quentin on my team so I could grow and improve. And I'm sure he'd say the same about me.

A word on wedding organisation

If you're living somewhere but organise your wedding in another place, learn to delegate. As Quentin and I were organising our wedding in Belgium from the UK, we obviously couldn't visit all the potential venues so we asked our mums to go instead. As for the rest, technology helped us choose the contractors for the catering, photography, flowers and music ourselves. We also chose the decorations, which weren't always met with approval from our families!

Make sure they trust your choices. In the end, it's your wedding and everything will be just fine.

Also, and I am talking about my own feelings, I think in some ways it might be easier to organise a wedding from afar. I have heard so many stories about families tearing each other apart. Being in separate countries means you won't see your family going crazy or make it easy for them to keep asking you annoying questions all the time.

On family and friends

When living abroad, don't assume it will be life as usual. You're going to miss a lot of things, and that's okay. But if you plan a long time ahead, you'll be there for the moments that matter the most.

Also, not all friendships will last the distance. You have got to cherish your most precious relationships and let go of others. But don't forget that you'll find amazing people along the way.

Addresses

Because I couldn't end this chapter on life without giving you my tips on where best to eat and what to visit, here's a condensed version of what you need to experience for yourself.

Eating & Drinking

Eat Tokyo

16 Old Compton Street, Soho, London W1D 4TL

I've had the best sushi of my life in Soho. You've got to book in advance though, because the restaurant is very popular and is located near the theatres.

Closest tube station? Tottenham Court Road.

Boulangerie Joie de Vie

359 Ballards Lane, North Finchley, London N12 8LJ

We were so happy when we found out about this French bakery! The lemon pies are to die for and we'd always love having lunch there. It's a bit far from Central London, but it's worth it.

Closest tube station? Woodside Park.

Exmouth Market

Exmouth Market, Farringdon, London EC1R 4QA

There are a couple of food markets across London, but if you have to experience one, you'd better go to Exmouth Market. It's Quentin approved – and he does love food.

Closest tube station? Farringdon.

Yumchaa Soho

45 Berwick St, Soho, London W1F 8SF

I learned to appreciate tea because of Yumchaa. They have a ton of different flavours, just pick one and discover the new fragrance. Hot or cold, you choose. And their matcha cake is simply delicious!

Closest tube station? Tottenham Court Road.

Pachamama

18 Thayer Street, Marylebone, London W1U 3JY

One of my friends, Ophélie, helped me discover Pachamama's Peruvian cuisine. The restaurant had beautiful decor and excellent food.

Closest tube station? Bond Street.

Tibits

12-14 Heddon St, Mayfair, London W1B 4DA

Tibits offers a vegan buffet that Quentin appreciated so much he went back there five times in a row. I'm not much of a vegan myself, but it was still good.

Closest tube station? Piccadilly Circus.

My Old Dutch

131-132 High Holborn, Holborn, London WC1V 6PS

Looking for something sweet? My Old Dutch makes excellent waffles and pancakes for anyone who decides it's never too late or too early to eat dessert.

Closest tube station? Holborn.

Waterstones Piccadilly

203-206 Piccadilly, St. James's, London W1J 9HD

The bookshop flagship store is somewhere I loved spending time reading, writing and meeting with friends. They have a top floor café in which you can stay and work a little.

Closest tube station? Piccadilly Circus.

Visiting

Richmond Park

East Sheen, London SW14 8LL

I love special parks, and the deer run free in this one. In Richmond Park, I recommend renting a bike and cycling around the huge green area. Guaranteed memories!

Closest train station? Mortlake – you'll have to take the train if you want to reach Richmond Park, or take the bus.

Hampstead Heath

Hampstead, London NW5 1QR

Closer to Central London but still a bit of a way out, Hampstead Heath offers a good view of the city and one of the best spots to chill during summer.

Closest tube station? Hampstead Heath or Gospel Oak.

Holland Park

Ilchester Place, Kensington, London W8 6LU

You'll love Holland Park's Japanese garden, it's so beautiful. It's the smallest park of the three I'm recommending in this list, but still worth a detour.

Closest tube station? Holland Park.

Victoria & Albert Museum

Cromwell Rd, Knightsbridge, London SW7 2RL

This is my favourite museum. Not only does it have one of the best collections of Tudor artefacts, but it also runs some of the best exhibitions I've seen in London.

Closest tube station? South Kensington.

Photographer's Gallery

16-18 Ramillies St, Soho, London W1F 7LW

It's not so well known to tourists, but you'll want to have a look at the Photographer's Gallery. They have amazing exhibitions, if you're passionate about photography in general... Quentin loved the place.

Closest tube station? Oxford Circus.

Tate Modern

Bankside, London SE1 9TG

The Tate Modern always had the weirdest exhibitions I have ever seen, which make you think about a ton of things. It's a really nice place to be and I highly recommend it.

Closest tube station? Southwark.

Southbank Centre

Belvedere Road, London SE1 8XX

For musical events, I'd like to introduce you to the Southbank Centre. Talented people from everywhere in the world perform there: you really don't want to miss it.

Closest tube station? Waterloo or Embankment (you'll have to cross a bridge over the Thames, though).

Somerset House

Somerset House, London WC2R 1LT

Art exhibitions and workshops are regularly organised at Somerset House. You'll want to have a look at their schedule before going, as you may find something interesting. And if you like architecture, the building is well worth a look.

Closest tube station? Temple.

Apps

Two precious apps I've used throughout my time in the UK were Citymapper and Trainline. Without their help, I think I'd have gotten lost more often.

- **Citymapper** helps you navigate the London public transports: buses, tubes and trains won't have any more secrets for you. There's also a map if you'd like to walk or cycle. I can't recommend it enough.

- **Trainline** saved our lives when we were in Brighton. There are so many train companies in the UK – and every single one has different fares – so you never know which one to take! Trainline centralises all the information you have to know to navigate the British train system... and saves you a lot of money in the process.

7. Brexit

They voted out

A small disclaimer before I start babbling on about the B-word: I'm not a political expert in any way. Britons voted "Leave" on the 24th June 2016 and effectively left the European Union on the 31st January 2020. I just happened to be in the UK during the referendum and a significant part of the negotiations with the EU. What you're about to read is my perspective, memories and opinion about the whole thing.

So, without further ado, let's talk about Brexit.

I hadn't paid attention to the campaign leading up to the referendum in June 2016 because, from what I had heard, Europeans living in the UK couldn't vote even if they wanted to. Brexit was all about Britons "giving back control". Control of their borders, in particular, because, as everyone knows, foreigners are taking all the good jobs (insert sarcastic sound here). From the bubble of my social media window, it seemed I didn't need to worry: Remainers couldn't lose the vote, right? It sounded impossible.

The morning of the 24th June 2016 will forever leave a mark. I looked at my phone just as I was waking up. My eyes shot wide open and panic rose in my chest. I reread the text message from my friend Justyna. Next to me, Quentin was still half asleep. As soon as the meaning of the message reached my brain, I shared the news with him. It was terrible: they had voted out.

"What does it mean for us?" I asked.

51.89% of the people had voted to leave the European Union. It was a close result but enough so the Prime Minister, David Cameron, who was broadly speaking pro-European, resigned to let Brexit – the choice of the people – happen. Enough so I would feel rejected by the country I had moved to a year before. Enough so that everyone had but one question on their lips: what's next?

Nobody knew.

After the result, journalists reported many stories of racism. Just because someone had a foreign name or a different skin colour, they were shouted at to "go back home". It was pure, unadulterated racism, as many of those people had been born in the country, the UK was their home and, for many of them, their residency status didn't depend in any way on the EU. These stories were terrifying.

I guess I'm lucky to have been born white. I'm lucky not to wear any visible religious signs. I'm lucky my face didn't have "foreigner" written all over it, so walking the streets was still safe for me. I measure my privilege for not being part of those stories.

Having succeeded David Cameron, Theresa May triggered Article 50 in March 2017. This meant the beginning of the withdrawal procedure from the EU, and the British parliament agreed to it. From an outsider's point of view, it looked like a bad dream from which everyone would surely wake up soon. Theresa May started negotiations with the EU, apparently without asking anyone's opinion on it. The agreement she had worked on would be rejected three times by parliament. This resulted in Brexit being pushed back a couple of times. She eventually resigned in July 2019, and was succeeded by Boris Johnson, former Mayor of London.

Brexit had many consequences.

Between June 2016 and July 2019, Europeans and Britons alike didn't know which way to turn. For many Europeans living in the UK, the fear of the unknown was almost unbearable. Many left the country.

The British economy slowly crashed. We had arrived in 2015, when the pound sterling had been strong. After Brexit, our salaries dropped in value. The UK wasn't an El Dorado after all. It wasn't the country I had thought it was: free, strong and majestic. We still found interesting and challenging jobs in London. But London isn't the whole country, even though you could think it is if you live there.

There was however a solution for Europeans living in the UK: citizenship. After five years, you'd be able to get it by filling in forms and proving your residency in the country for the past five years.

Did Brexit influence our decision to leave the UK? Certainly.

However, saying that Brexit was the main reason for our departure would be a lie. Quentin and I had already been thinking about our next move as a couple – more on that in the next chapter.

Brexit got pushed back one more time to the 31st January 2020. But this time, it went through for good. A sad day for us as expats.

It is March 2020 as I'm writing these lines and I still can't believe that a country such as the UK decided to leave. The racism and bigotry shown by a few has destroyed the place of the UK inside the European Union.

Through lies and broken promises, some politicians and journalists have achieved what they wanted. But at what cost? Only time can tell.

What you need to know

What does Brexit change for you? Will you need a passport, a visa, a work permit? I'm giving you some useful resources, but I can't talk from personal experience.

If you're coming from overseas

The rules that applied in the past are currently still in operation. You still need a visa and a passport to enter the country. You still need to get a work permit to get a job. Everything you need to know is listed on the UK government website: https://www.gov.uk/topic/immigration-operational-guidance

If you're coming from Europe

Before Brexit, you only needed an ID card to travel to the UK. After Brexit, however, the rules are changing. You'll need a passport to visit the country, and you'll have a few more rules that apply whether or not you want to stay and work. At this stage, I can't get you any valid information. I suggest you have a look on the UK government website once you decide you'd like to make the jump.

Europeans who are already in the UK can apply to the EU settlement scheme until June 2021. But if you decide to stay after June 2021, maybe you'd like to apply for citizenship. You can obtain more information on the topic here: https://www.gov.uk/british-citizenship

8. Moving Back

Going back to our roots

I've never felt much of a patriot. Before I even considered moving to the UK, my opinion of my home country was fairly low, to say the least. It was the beginning of my career, the beginning of my adult life and I was struggling. But once I moved out of Belgium, I started feeling proud of my little country; proud of the culture and food, proud of the people.

After four years in the UK, I finally understood what it was to have roots. It gave me a sense of community I hadn't really had a grasp of before. However, Quentin and I had built our lives in London. We had found a good place, jobs and amazing friends. How could we possibly want to move back to Belgium?

After we got married in October 2017, we wanted to move on to the next stage of our life together: buying a house – crazy expensive in London! – and starting a family – which we were sure would cost us a kidney and I wouldn't have wanted to do it without my mum by my side anyway. Some people can afford buying a house and having a family – it would be sad otherwise – but we didn't think we could.

Another reason was that I wanted to spend time with my grandparents. They had moved to a new house, closer to my mum's so she could take care of them. However, they were getting older by the day.

But you know us by now, don't you? We were still considering moving elsewhere, maybe to another city in the UK or to another country altogether. I was pushing for Belgium though. In my heart, it felt like the best decision: going back to our roots.

By early August 2018, we had made up our minds.

"Let's move in a year's time," we agreed.

I had the perfect plan: I would train myself until January, learning Dutch and Google Ads, then I'd update my CV and covering letter and start applying for jobs. On his side, Quentin had a high chance of being able to keep his London job. He did end up keeping it for one more year after we moved.

In mid-December 2018, I came across a job opportunity: a Belgian company near Brussels was looking for a content manager. I applied right away, but never thought I'd find a job that easily. They set up an interview a couple of days after my application. I remember I was recovering from the flu when I talked with them for the first time. I finished a writing test on the train back to Belgium for the Christmas holiday and got the final interview the very next day at their office.

They offered me the job on Boxing Day 2018.

After everything that had happened, and the struggle I endured to find a permanent role in London, I was stunned. It was all going so fast. We had planned to move back in the summer but they wanted me to start as soon as possible, that is, in March 2019.

"I'll have to tell Richard," I panicked.

How could I do that to him, to the team, to the company? I felt so sad and ungrateful for the chance they had given me. Richard and the team had become my family, I dreaded their reactions.

"It's a big company, they'll get over it," Quentin said.

He was right, of course.

I handed in my resignation on the 7th January 2019, as soon as I sat at my desk, back from holiday.

"Can I talk to you for a second?" I texted my direct manager, Michael, a tall Australian guy.

I could see on his face he was expecting what I was going to tell him. He was just waiting for the wave to hit the shore. We sat down together in the office kitchen. I looked around, thinking about how I'd miss these colourful chairs once I was gone.

"My husband and I have decided to move back to our country. And I got a job offer," I explained.

Because we had a project and were progressing towards completing it, my colleagues' reaction wasn't that bad. My last day was quickly determined: the 7th March 2019. I was turning yet another page in my life.

We announced our departure to our London friends as soon as I resigned, telling them that the move was happening sooner than we had thought. Hugs were involved. No tears though, we knew better. When you're an expat in such a big city, you know it's only for a set period of time. You create strong bonds with other expats but you know, deep down, that they're going to leave. You also know that, with today's technology, you'll be able to nurture those relationships wherever you're going, if you truly want to.

But we weren't starting over. Our close family and friends were super happy to welcome us back. And we already had a place where we could stay for a time until we were able to buy our own house.

So how did we move back?

Remember that at the beginning of our adventure, Quentin and I had crossed the Channel Tunnel with one suitcase each. Needless to say that, after all these years in the UK, we had accumulated things. Not a crazy amount though, because when you move houses a lot – and we moved pretty much every year – you tend to "Marie Kondo" your life. If you don't know, Marie Kondo is the creator of the

KonMari method, a system of simplifying and organising your home by getting rid of physical items that don't bring joy into your life.

So I rolled up my sleeves and checked exactly what we would need to carry back to Belgium. The furniture was out of the question, because Brexit was about to happen, precisely at the moment we were supposed to be moving back, March 2019. We didn't want to take the risk of renting a van and getting stuck at the border.

Anyway, I realised we had way too many things. The books, for instance, were so heavy and there were so many of them that I panicked.

"We'll never succeed! How are we going to make it?" I cried.

"We'll find a solution, don't worry too much," Quentin said, consoling a tiny Estelle huddled up in the corner of the sofa.

Am I the type of person who worries a lot? Oh, definitely. But fortunately, we had family coming over in January. We gave them as many books as possible to carry for us. I will always remember the look on my sister Elaine's face when she saw the huge bag of books she had to carry on the Eurostar. We sold the rest of the furniture by advertising them on Facebook groups. Bit by bit, our London flat was being emptied while our Belgian place was getting furnished.

My mum visited us in this period of limbo. The only thing that had changed was that I would be going back with her, with a lot of suitcases. It wasn't as sad as when we had crossed the sea to come to a foreign country though. This time we were going home.

While I was getting used to Belgian life, having started the new job on the 11th March 2019, Quentin was still in London preparing for the transition. He was living with less and less furniture, while getting out of the house as much as possible not to see the sadness surrounding the place. He finally moved back to Belgium a month after me.

We had to register as residents again. Even though it was our birth country, it doesn't mean we were exempted. A year before us, it had been the turn of Sophie, who was now my sister-in-law.

"It's incredible how slow the whole process is!" she had explained. "They're not prepared, they're silly and incompetent. You'll have to wait for hours before they finally understand what they have to do to register you back in their files."

Even though I was dreading doing it, I had to do it anyway. The sooner, the better.

Having reached the Town Hall of the Belgian city I was now living in, I entered and queued for five minutes. It was a tall, grey building I hadn't seen in ages. The whole process of registering me back in the Belgian files took five more minutes and a neighbourhood officer came to check that I was living in the new place one or two days afterward.

"Wasn't so bad in the end," I thought.

It's a particular feeling when you end an adventure. We had achieved so much in the four years we had lived in the UK. Those four years will certainly leave a mark in our hearts for the rest of our lives.

"Oh, you're back. Where did you go?" Quentin's grandma would say, when we visited.

"London, grandma," he answered.

"But did you speak English?"

Some things never change.

What you need to know

Time to move out? There are two options for you: either you're moving to your country of origin, or you're pursuing a new adventure in a new country. If it's the latter, you have got to do everything all over again. New phone number, new bank account, new job, new house, etc. If you're going back home, well... it's the same but in a familiar way!

Starting a new job

If you're lucky enough to start a new job at the same time as moving, be careful. For example, you have got to work for a year in Belgium before you can claim your holidays. I had been warned but didn't listen, which resulted in me not having paid days off for a year. Even though I had been working in the UK... it still wasn't Belgium. I wish I had listened, as I would have taken a holiday before leaving my London position. So my general advice here is: know what you're stepping into beforehand. And take at least a week off before you start your new job.

Preparing for a new adventure?

What if you're choosing to move country again? Now that you know what expatriation entails, you have all the basic information in hand to make decisions though of course you will still need to check local rules.

Just don't forget to be yourself at all times, and to get the most out of your experience.

Every adventure has an end, or has it?

I never thought I'd live through such an incredible experience.

Living in a foreign country taught me a lot: how to live with someone, how to dream big, how to never give up and how to open my mind to different cultures. London was undoubtedly the perfect place to be. Everything the world has to offer was gathered in one city.

I loved my London life. If I had to do it all over again, I would do it in a flash.

At the beginning of our adventure, our biggest fear was that we would come back to Belgium and end up living as if nothing had happened, then feel stuck again. If you had asked our mums, they would have said that they'd feared for us wandering off.

Living in London, in a city where nobody knew us, was like living in a bubble. Expatriation means you've got to start over, make new friends, and build a life. Our Belgian friends and family had become a lifeline which we came back to when we were feeling homesick.

Quentin and I had both achieved so much during those four years. We struggled and won together. It taught us we could count on one another, more than we had ever known.

Our experience opened doors to many opportunities on a professional level. Having "London" written on a CV made it easier for us to get new jobs in Belgium. It showed that we had gone outside our comfort zone to seek the best experience.

We have now come back to our home country. The difference this time is that we have chosen this life. I think this is important to mention and to highlight that word: choose. Not only had we chosen to leave but we had also chosen to come back.

This is a pretty powerful thought.

I had taken Belgium for granted during my whole life before I left. Being an expat opened my heart to my country, something that wouldn't have happened before – I had felt so lost. But once you choose to live somewhere, you do it freely.

We are now living in a two-storey house near our families. The space is gigantic compared to our $42m^2$ London flat. We even have a garden!

Coming back to Belgium allowed me to spend some time with my grandparents before the end, which is time I'll always be grateful for. Now, it's up to us to start our own family.

Life in Belgium is a bit different, but not that much so. We have come back to our families and we have found exciting opportunities. But when people hear we've lived in London, they always ask "don't you miss it?" The answer is: not really.

Belgium and the UK aren't that far from each other, neither are they so different. We've learnt we can travel for one or two hours to attend an event or visit our friends – going to work involved crossing the whole city sometimes, haha. And whenever I set foot at St-Pancras International, my eyes sparkle.

Once a Londoner, always a Londoner.

If you ever consider making the jump, go ahead and do it! You'll never regret that experience, and I think it'll open your eyes to so many things. All will be worth it, as long as you're doing it in the right conditions, for the right reasons and at the right time.

Wherever you go, I am sure it's the start of a fantastic adventure. And I can't wait to hear all about it.

Printed in Great Britain
by Amazon